WANTED

Nobody is ever without hope!

E L L I S   L U C A S

ISBN 978-1-7332656-0-7 (Paperback)
ISBN 978-1-7332656-1-4 (Digital)

Cover design by Kristine Cotterman, Exodus Design Studio

Published by Pearl Press
6350 Vail Circle
Colorado Springs, CO, 80919

Divine intervention led to my finding my younger biological brother Ellis Lucas and three younger sisters Debbie, Jeanne, and Brenda on January 22, 2017. Shortly thereafter, Ellis's divinely inspired writing led me to finding the Lord! If you are struggling with your faith or are just outright lost, *Wanted* as well as *The Potter and the Clay* are both inspirational testimonies of a man whose trials may reflect your own. In this book, Ellis reveals the story behind the story, offering an inside look at the personal relationship between himself and God that resulted in Ellis being saved and restored. Twenty years after his day of salvation, God, in His providence, orchestrated the events that opened the door for my own day of salvation—a miracle that followed the miracle of my finding my family, my biological brother, and three younger sisters that I had never known, met, or even knew existed until January 22, 2017!

—Rob Reese

My life changed two years ago when I met Ellis and Peggi Lucas. They showed me the true way to glory through Jesus Christ more than anyone else in my adult life. I grew up going to church and thought I knew Jesus Christ. I knew who He was, I believed He was the Son of God, but I did not *know* Him! Ellis and Peggi helped me with that. Ellis's knowledge of the Scriptures has helped to bring me closer to Jesus and has inspired me to spend more time reading my Bible.

Ellis is my close brother in Christ, but it wasn't until after I read *The Potter and the Clay*, Ellis's autobiography, that I really began to know Ellis Lucas—the person, the pain, the struggles, the defeats, the bruises, and the brokenness that I never would have guessed he had experienced. That book really touched my heart, igniting a desire within me to put my trust completely in Jesus Christ. The Lord has taught me so much through abiding in His Word and following where He leads. And today, I know my Lord because He made Himself known to me!

The Potter and the Clay is an inspirational story of one man's amazing journey from devastating hopelessness to glory and paradise after a life-changing encounter with Jesus. *Wanted* is as equally inspirational and gives a detailed account of the process which resulted in the transformation written about in *The Potter and the Clay* that made Ellis the man he is today.

If you think your life is hopeless, then I strongly encourage you to read *Wanted*. You will never see yourself the same way again, as this quote from inside this book says, "What God has created out of the broken pieces of my life before knowing Jesus Christ is a tremendous example for why no one, for any reason, should ever compromise their heart's conviction. We don't have to accept failure, give in to loneliness or isolation or low self-esteem, get weighted down with feelings of being unwanted or unloved or unworthy or rejected, or ever settle for defeat." Amen!

—Ed Lococo

Wanted offers a personal look into the life-changing effects of salvation. Ellis Lucas effectively demonstrates what it means to be a genuine follower of Christ, offering examples from his own life and supplementing every point he makes with a scriptural basis. His passion to share the Gospel with the lost and broken is truly inspiring and offers a genuine look into the power of witnessing, trusting God in the hard times, and following through with His plan for your life. After reading Ellis's book, you'll feel personally challenged to not only reignite your spiritual journey, but also to get out of your comfort zone and reach the lost.

—A. E. Schwartz, Christian author and editor

Each week, I visit people in jail or former inmates; addicts in recovery. I see great discouragement, darkness, and pain in their lives. Entering the battle for the soul is not negotiable; you and I will face spiritual warfare in our everyday lives! We need each other. We need the love and grace of Jesus Christ every day. And once again, Ellis Lucas has written a book that speaks spiritual truth into the hearts of people suffering from addiction, abandonment, and abuse.

In a very real sense, addiction recovery is a foundational soul-need of all mankind, for we are all prone to be prideful, hard-hearted, and stiff-necked. We often rush ahead without seeking God's best; we act out habitual selfish plans and desires. Ellis's latest book, *Wanted*, invites the reader to come home to Jesus Christ and enter that secret place of the humbled heart where Jesus waits for each of us. Ellis gives solid Scriptural reasons to seek and follow in Jesus's footsteps. Practical, believable, true-life stories about real people inspire the reader to seek the Lord and make healthy choices.

After reading Ellis's book *Wanted*, I felt spiritually encouraged and was inspired to spend more time in the presence of Jesus. As the reader, you will also be refreshed, feeling motivated to step deeper into the river of God's amazing love and the truth of His Word. May the Holy Spirit comfort and bless you as you intentionally seek more of Jesus in your life-walk."

—Fred Carlson, Founder of True Friends Place in Mora, MN. Also, Founder of Rehab & Recovery, a mentorship community for people recovering from drug addiction and incarceration

I've known Ellis for almost three years. It's very obvious to me that Christ has done a major work in his life. This book helped clarify why his walk is so strong. Sharing his experiences was a great tool in bringing across the scriptural message that was burning in his heart. I enjoyed this book very much. I found it very refreshing and encouraging!

—John Schlitt, lead singer for the rock bands Head East, Petra, and Union of the Sinners and the Saints

"May the words of my mouth and the meditation of my heart be acceptable to You, Lord, my rock and my Redeemer" (Ps. 19:14). This is the passion of Ellis Lucas. He is a man that loves the Lord and loves to share the Word of the Lord. Ellis's heart is to use his salvation story as a vehicle to reach the lost. With *Wanted*, he wants the world to know that, as the Lord Jesus Christ—his Rock, his Redeemer, the one Who has set him free—changed his heart and restored the shattered pieces of his broken past, the same is also readily available to all who call on the name of Jesus Christ. Ellis gives solid scriptural as well as testimonial evidence for why we can hope for and believe for so much more than even salvation beginning the moment we open the door for Jesus Christ to become Lord of our lives. It all comes down to a choice—either accepting the Jesus of the Bible or rejecting the truth and never experiencing the true life that was prepared by God in advance for you. Ellis's own life gives credence to what Paul said in 2 Corinthians 2:9: "Eye has not seen, nor ear heard, nor have entered into the heart of man the things which God has prepared for those who love Him." Another great book!

—Rev. John Mohler, Pastor and Evangelist,
KC Chapter Elder for Bikers for Christ

God delights in you. Yes, you. And you. And even you. I know what some of you might be thinking, "He *delights* in me? How can this be when even *I* don't delight in me?" Maybe you've messed up. Maybe you've ruined something—again. Maybe you feel like you've been a screwup your entire life. Guess what? God still delights in you. How can I know? Because this is the same God Who spoke the universe into existence. He has named every single star and put the planets on their axis. He blinked, and the mountains were formed; sighed, and the depths of the ocean were carved out. He filled the atmosphere with the perfect amount of oxygen. He put into motion everything from whales to ants. But the only thing He put His breath into was *you*.

You are not a copy of anyone else. If your life, your meaning, your purpose, or your worth wasn't anything to God, He would have busted out the cookie cutter a long time ago and saved Himself some time. But that's not how our God rolls. He remembers sewing your specific fingerprint onto your fingertips. He remembers forming your voice box and crafting the unique sound only you create. He remembers mixing together your DNA that is unlike any of the other billions upon billions of humans to live. He numbered every single hair on your head. For some of you, that was easier than others, but that's not the point. The point is this: God uniquely created you, not because He could, but because He desired too.

He has been fighting since the beginning of time to show you just how much He loves you. Zephaniah 3:17 says, "For the Lord your God is living among you. He is a mighty savior. He will take delight in you with gladness. With His love, He will calm all your fears. He will rejoice over you with joyful songs" (NLT). God is so happy with you that Scripture literally says He is singing and dancing over you right now. 1 John 3:1 says, "See how very much our Father loves us, for He calls us children, and that is what we are!" (NLT). You were created to be His child—His son, His daughter. His prince and princess. His masterpiece. His prized possession. His ultimate creation. You are worthy. You are valued. You are delighted in. You are *loved*. You are *wanted*!

—Pastor Evan Stone, Student Life Pastor,
Mountain Springs Church

I want to begin by dedicating this book to the true author, Jesus Christ, Who formed me and redeemed me by sacrificing His own life in my place on Calvary's Cross. Thank You, Lord Jesus, for everything. I pray You are pleased and honored with this project! I love You!

CONTENTS

Foreword...13

Acknowledgments 15

Introduction...19

Chapter 1:   The Unknown God...27
Chapter 2:   God's Most Wanted..40
Chapter 3:   All That Is in the World 51
Chapter 4:   A Bruised Reed He Will Not Break 57
Chapter 5:   Love Thy Enemies..66
Chapter 6:   Whom Shall I Send,
                   Who Will Go for Us? 75
Chapter 7:   Delight Yourself Also in the Lord 86
Chapter 8:   It Is Not Good for Man to Be Alone!.......................99
Chapter 9:   Faith without Works Is Dead.................................111
Chapter 10: Identity Crisis...123
Chapter 11: The Price Is Right 133
Chapter 12: Iron Sharpens Iron II
                   Part I: Faith, Hope, and Love 144
Chapter 13: Iron Sharpens Iron II
                   Part II: The Morning After.....................................149
Chapter 14: Who Do Men Say I Am?.....................................158
Chapter 15: The Spirit and the Bride Say, "Come." 168

FOREWORD

The undersigned has known Ellis Lucas for many years, ministered in his church, had fellowship with him, and know his life, his testimony, his example as a Christian leader, and his compassion for others. It all comes across in this book. In addition to the main premise, it will challenge Christians to do everything they can to reach those who are considered by many as "unreachable."

In reading the manuscript of this book, there were so many different things that "jumped out" at me that caused me to wish I would have had this book in my hand to give to many people over the past sixty-two years of ministry (the last forty-four of that in a multicultural, inner-city church), who honestly believed they were hopeless: people who were bound and enslaved by so many things, people who felt crushed by life, people who had been abused and abandoned, and so many who felt totally unloved and were sure that God couldn't care about them. Many people feel that "if there is a God, I've gone too far away from Him and done too many things that He could never forgive me, and He certainly doesn't want me. There is no hope…*I'm not wanted.*"

The personal testimony of Ellis Lucas and the testimonies of others he shares give living proof that God loves *you*; regardless of where you have been or what you have done, God not only loves you and *wants you*, but He is also able to take your life and totally turn it around and make you a living witness of His love, grace, and power to change the life of anyone who comes to Him.

Another thing that "jumped out" at me when I read it is the constant flow of Scripture like a mighty river backing up everything. Readers will not only be told by the testimonies that God loves and wants them, but they will hear it loud and clear from the Bible itself, God saying, "I love you and, oh yes, you are wanted."

George W. Westlake Jr., D. Min
Pastor Emeritus
Sheffield Family Life Center, Kansas City, Missouri

ACKNOWLEDGMENTS

To the love of my life and best friend forever, my beautiful wife, Peggi Sue. Thank you, sweetheart, for all your help with this book as well as the last, and for making my life so exciting and wonderful. I love you more than life!

I don't want to forget these three awesome young grandsons, Tyler McCandlish, Christopher McCandlish, and Kory Rushing! God loves you guys and so do I!

Also, my brother, Rob Reese; his wife, Darla; their family and our three sisters; Brenda Kemper—a true reflection of our late mother; Debbie Peterson; Jeanne Buntin; their families; and, of course, our precious mother, Mary Jeannette Lucas; and my wonderful friend and dad, Dean Lucas. Also, to our two forever beautiful cousins, Mary Bolton Reyna and Linda Roffall, and all their amazing South Texas family members—Peggi and I love you dearly!

I am truly honored to include a very special brother and sister in the Lord, Tom and Karen Heun. I have learned so much from both of you, and what is always evident in both of you is a genuine Christ-centered heart that is simply above approach and honorable in every way! Thank you for modeling true faithfulness to Christ and others, especially in an age when faithfulness is a rare commodity. You are the light of the world, that city on a hill that cannot be hidden. Peg and I love you and cherish your friendship more than words could ever say!

To Randy and Lillian Carter. Thank you for fulfilling a personal dream of singing and recording with me. I will cherish this special treasure for all of eternity. Love you guys!

I also want to dedicate this book to Nancy Redmond, a special friend from my hometown in Stanberry, Missouri. Thank you, Nancy, for showing us how true faith in Christ and courage are real and unbreakable, especially under the most difficult circumstances. We love you, and you're the best!

To John Mohler, the remarkable John Silva, and our faithful Bikers for Christ family! Thank you all so much. We love you, and God bless you all!

I celebrate the life of one of God's mighty prayer intercessors, Loreta Jean Adams. "Jean" went home to be with Jesus just four months prior to what would have been her one hundredth birthday (October 1, 1917 – June 18, 2017). I owe this precious lady such a great debt of gratitude, and am honored to honor her in the dedications of this book! Thank you, Jean, for everything! I love and miss you but celebrate your amazing life and reward in Christ!

I want to include a giant thank-you to Ashley Schwartz for doing such an amazing job editing this book, for your counsel and encouragement and patience. Thanks, Ashley!

I want to thank three great men of God who have left an indelible impression on my life since becoming a Christian—Dr. George Westlake Jr. of Sheffield Family Life Center in Kansas City, Missouri; Pastor Steve Poe, Sr. Pastor of Northview Church in Carmel; and my close friend and mentor, David Lin! Thank you all so much for sowing a part of your lives into mine. I love and appreciate you all very, very much!

A very special dedication to Jason Ferris of Bread of Stone and Skylar Kaylyn, a remarkable young songwriter/recording artist—both of whom met at a 2014 His Heart United event in Castle Rock, Colorado, fell in love, and were united in Holy Matrimony this past May of 2017. So special, and how sweet it is! Peggi and I love you both and wish you the absolute best future and tremendous life in loving each other and loving our Jesus!

Thanks also to my wonderful friend John Schlitt for setting such an unprecedented example in humility and genuine heart to serve others. Also, for all you have sown into my life personally and for representing our Savior's eternal kingdom with such remarkable class. Jesus is so pleased with you, John, and I am beyond honored to have you for a friend and eternal brother!

A million thanks to Kristine Cotterman of Exodus Web and Design Studio for doing such a stellar job with *The Potter and the Clay* and *Wanted* designs, and my new author website! May God reward your time and tremendous contribution - https://www.exodusdesign.com.

And then finally, to one of my young heroes of the faith, Hunter Mix, the son of a very dear friend and brother in Christ, Dennis Mix. As of the writing of this book, Hunter had just turned nineteen years old and has already been around the world laying down his young life for the opportunity to share the Gospel with people who have never heard the name of Jesus before. Here is a brief word from Hunter, written while serving deep in the jungles of Africa:

> I never thought I would grow to love these people so much. They're all so kind and hospitable, yet they are still in darkness, so I love them all the more. Do not worry about me because I am in God's hands, and I'm carrying the greatest news in the world to people who do not yet know it or believe it. I am certain that this is a cause worth sacrificing my life for.
>
> "I now rejoice in my sufferings for you, and fill up in my flesh what is lacking in the afflictions of Christ, for the sake of His body, which is the church" (Col. 1:24)! "For though I am absent in the flesh, yet I am with you in spirit, rejoicing to see your good order and the steadfastness of your faith in Christ" (Col. 2:5). Amen! Love you all! (Hunter Mix)

INTRODUCTION

What is the first thing you think of when you hear the word *wanted*? An old Western movie with some outlaw's face posted on a wanted poster? Perhaps America's Most Wanted? Both would be understandable answers, according to Webster's and most other modern dictionaries that have *fugitive* or *wanted by the law* at or near the top of their descriptive definitions. And undoubtedly, we are living in an age where lawlessness continues to spread around the globe like a native green tree planted by the water's edge, where evil men and imposters continue to increasingly deceive and be deceived, and where many innocent kids and adults alike have been crushed in the wake of this latter-day storm. Trust betrayed, vows forsaken, addictions, suicide, abuse, and depression have destroyed many families, resulting in a world in crisis.

Here in America, we are living in a postmodern era where truth is considered subjective. In other words, truth is relative to one's viewpoint. What's true for one may not be true for another in an age where truth revolves around tolerance, meaning that truth is no longer accepted as objective, absolute, universal, or fixed. And instead of asking, "Is it right or true?" society today, regardless of the consequences, spontaneously reacts to "does it make me feel good?" It's self-centered, uncivilized, and socially and spiritually destructive. Feelings are far more important to postmodernists than acknowledging the reality of truth. Consequently, they use music, images, films, stories, plays—you name it—to express their feelings, fully understanding how people are more easily influenced when their emotions are tapped into. And with smart phones, computers, and the World Wide Web, postmodernism has left an indelible mark on the lives of this generation here in America as well as around the world.

Jesus, when talking about the end of this age, said there would be a time when many would fall away and betray one another and hate one another. In that time many false teachers would arise and deceive many (Matt. 24:10–11). We are witnessing the most intolerable conflict of this age erupting between liberals and conservatives, an emotional civil war where truth varies between America's founding historical Christian world view and modern secularism. Lies and deceit have filled the air causing a bitter division all around the world that has spread like a cancer well beyond the sphere of the public arena to dividing individual families and the body of Christ.

One of the most noticeable differences in the culture I grew up in and the culture today is how much lawlessness has increased and how so many once-God-fearing people's love has waxed cold as Jesus predicted would happen (Matt. 24:12)! We are now living in those perilous final times that Paul predicted when society would become lovers of themselves, lovers of money, boasters, proud, blasphemers, disobedient to parents, unthankful, unholy, unloving, unforgiving, slanderers, without self-control, brutal, despisers of good, traitors, headstrong, haughty, lovers of pleasure rather than lovers of God, having a form of godliness but denying its power (2 Tim. 3:2–5).

Since the release of *The Potter and the Clay*, my autobiography in 2014, I've heard the cries of the forgotten members of society, I feel the unending pain, and I've seen tears flowing out from the depths of human despair where comes the issues of life pouring out from the heart fed reservoirs. Hearts cut deep and badly broken by the realization of the high cost and consequences of moral compromise. So today, when I hear the word *wanted*, I think about a world of broken human lives, wounded and forsaken, abandoned and rejected, abused and isolated, feeling unloved, unwanted, and hopeless. And although the emotional stress of this present dark age is very real and, at times, mentally overwhelming, nothing could be further from the truth.

Studies have shown that when people do experience an unnatural degree of loss, rejection, or neglect, it is a natural reaction for them to internalize incredible fear and anxiety, resulting in a badly diminished degree of self-worth and confidence while creating long-term complications with suspicion and trust, fear and faith, an emotional imbalance creating a mental war within us which equals unhealthy relationships and broken homes. Not receiving the necessary spiritual, emotional, intimate, and physical support can and does equal what is defined as abandonment, "the act by which a person abandons and forsakes, without justification, a condition of public, social, or family life, renouncing its responsibilities and evading its duties." And while just one actual experience with abandonment can cause complicated long-term emotional struggles, repeated abandonment experiences can create a very toxic form of mental shame that can result in deadly consequences.

Shame often arises from a very painful emotional message implied in abandonment: "You're not important, you're of no value, and sadly, you're not *wanted*!" People begin to wrestle with the question, "Is life worth living?" This is a serious conflict where peace and freedom depend on truth, and victory and healing are a result of absolution. But when anger turns to despair and despair turns to hopelessness, emotions equal torment and pain, and sadly, it's a false narrative designed with the intent of destruction. This is a serious problem of epidemic proportions and a very painful reality from which countless people of all ages and every culture need to heal.

The purpose in my writing this book is to expose the fallacy of Satan's intentional mental warfare designed to crush the spirit and decrease the stability of our minds. But just before Jesus ascended to our Father's house to prepare a place for us, He said, "You did not choose Me, but I chose you and appointed you that you should go and bear fruit, and that your fruit should remain, that whatever you ask the Father in My name He may give you. These things I command you, that you love one another" (John 15:16–17, NKJV)! "I have said these things to you, that in Me you may have peace. In the world you will have tribulation. But take heart; I have overcome the world" (John 16:33, NKJV). And because of Jesus's atoning work on Mount Calvary's cross we too can overcome this present dark age to find hope and healing for our wounded lives and love for our broken hearts. "For whatever is born of God overcomes the world. And this is the victory that has overcome the world—our faith" (1 John 5:4, NKJV)!

Satan is the master at mental warfare and has had plenty of time to master his craft. What's more, he is the accuser of the brethren (Rev. 12:10), but he doesn't stop there. I was always told that Satan isn't the slightest bit concerned with those whom society has written off as hopeless outcasts: inner city gang members, prostitutes, drug addicts, or that mentally deranged demon-possessed madman. Not so! Satan is not only concerned about these members of society, but he also fully understands how they can pose the greatest threat toward exposing his phony agenda, an agenda that only works when we believe his lies. When he speaks a lie, he speaks from his own resources, for he is a liar and the father of it (John 8:44b, NKJV). It's a battle of the mind wherein true faith in Jesus Christ is an impenetrable shield with which you will be able to quench all the fiery darts of the wicked one (Eph. 6:16). The helmet of salvation will protect or shield your heart, conscience and mind, and the sword of the Spirit, which is the word of God, will transform and renew your mind (Eph. 6:17).

But beware, when Satan begins to lose his grip and the shackles of lust or addiction begin to come undone because one of these outcasts becomes wise to his evil plot and repents, you will begin to see an enormous amount of strange activity which is yet another telltale sign that Satan is very nervous about that person. He will influence old friends, our former companions while we were in the world. The goal is to manipulate our emotions by creating a counterfeit compassion knowing where we are most vulnerable, exploiting our need for loving human relationships, human affection, support, and understanding. It's a difficult matter to discern, especially when kindness and deception wrap themselves around our storm-tossed emotions that crave peace and comfort. It's dangerous and deceptive, "and no wonder," says the Apostle Paul, "for even Satan disguises himself as an angel of light. So it is no surprise if his servants, also, disguise themselves as servants of righteousness. Their end will correspond to their deeds" (2 Cor. 11:14–15, ESV)!

James 1:14 says each one is tempted when he is drawn away by his own desires and enticed. But in this book, you will discover what transpires in our lives when we anchor ourselves to the truth in

God's word and leave the burden of proving it wrong on Satan. Three things will inevitably happen in the process; you will come to a transforming knowledge of the truth which will set you free from fear and bondage. That knowledge will result in you falling in love with and hungering for a personal relationship with Jesus Christ. And within that love you will discover the mercies of God, and strongly desire to present your body a living sacrifice, holy, acceptable to God, which is your reasonable service. You will joyfully abandon the destructive practices of this world which amount to sin and rebellion and no longer be conformed to this world, but instead be transformed by the renewing of your mind and ultimately prove what is that good and acceptable and perfect will of God (Rom. 12:1–2, NKJV). "Therefore," says Paul, "take up the whole armor of God, that you may be able to withstand in the evil day, and having done all, to stand. Stand therefore, having girded your waist with truth, having put on the breastplate of righteousness, and having shod your feet with the preparation of the gospel of peace" (Eph. 6:13–15, NKJV). You have this promise, that no weapon formed against you can or ever will prosper (Isa. 54:17)!

Satan knows how transformed lives like these are difficult to account for and have caused many unbelievers to trust in Christ! He still remembers the millions of hearts all around the world that were awakened by the former demoniac in Mark chapter five, Saul of Tarsus whose name was changed to Apostle Paul after his conversion, Mary Magdalene a former prostitute, John Newton the slave trader, and pastors and evangelists like, Dwight L. Moody, Charles H. Spurgeon broken vessels who encountered a transforming power through faith in Jesus Christ and were endued with an audacious courage and boldness that impacted cultures and communities, rural countrysides and urban cities in various nations and even the entire world in the process.

In *Wanted*, you will see just how audacious different former wounded outcasts had become, including me, and why there is everything to hope for and live for as God's workmanship created in Christ Jesus for the good works which God foreordained for them to walk in (Eph. 2:10). And while pain, failure, and rejection are a genuine reality for many people today, remember, your story is still being written and defeat is simply unnecessary. "There is no more condemnation for those who are in Christ Jesus. For the law of the Spirit of life in Christ Jesus has set you free from the law of sin and of death" (Rom. 8:1–2). "The Lord (Christ Jesus) is the Spirit, and where the Spirit of the Lord is, there is liberty" (2 Cor. 3:17, NASB)!

Yet, in any case, before I proceed, I want to say welcome and hello. My name is Ellis Lucas, and it is such a privilege and a tremendous honor to be able to share with you what is my hope in glory, Christ Jesus. I pray you will find this book to be deeply inspiring as you encounter the infinite grace, love, power, and mercy of God in Christ Jesus at work in and through the lives of some of society's most unlikely members of various societies, that it will ignite a fiery passion in your heart to vigorously seek and pursue that purpose for which you, too, were created!.

My books, *The Potter and the Clay* and *Wanted,* deal with the human suffering, addiction, abuse, rejection, anxiety, and depression that many of us endure, and the healing and overcoming we can experience when we place our trust in our savior and Lord, our Father's Son, Jesus Christ. I suffered greatly, through broken relationships, crippling addictions, spending numerous weekends in different county jails, and endured the intense pain of rejection and malicious gossip because of the reputation that preceded me. I was despised by nearly everyone who knew anything about me and for good reason. And for over two decades I was convinced that even God didn't love me and there was no hope for Heaven or salvation for me. But God, Who is rich in mercy and abounds in grace, set the record straight and filled my heart, conscience, and mind with a personal assurance of His never-ending love for me, and it changed my life forever. Like clay, we are crafted by the hands that hold us, cherish us and mold us, but we make our own conscious decisions in a world full of vices that are simply impossible to escape without the power of Christ's redeeming love.

My life reflects the deep learning lessons in how deferring to God will serve as a continuous life preserver for the wounded souls sinking in the troubled waters of hopelessness; empowering them to take back control of their individual destinies. In this empowerment comes transformation as we surrender completely to Christ—who suffered for us all, and sincerely from the heart—we are enabled to overcome impossible situations, pain, sin, and failures, and experience real healing for our bruised spirits and broken hearts that enable God to replant, cultivate, and nurture the seeds of hope and purpose deep inside of us and all around. In this healing, God transforms life's lonely deserts of isolation, depression, and shattered dreams into a joyous green fruitful life, giving us "beauty for ashes, the oil of joy for mourning, the garment of praise for the spirit of heaviness; that they, meaning the redeemed of the Lord, may be called trees of righteousness, the planting of the Lord, that He may be glorified" (Isa. 61:3, NKJV)!

My story is a story of great pain, but also one of great healing. It represents the truest divide in life, the chasm that separates the lost and wounded sinner from those healed and redeemed in Christ. My strong belief is that suffering has been my greatest teacher and it can be the gateway to transformation for you as well—as God's gift not only to us as individuals, but to inspire us to *inspire others* and inspire the world! In His name, Jesus Christ, as He did for us on a cross over two thousand years ago—and continues to do through the Holy Spirit today.

Charles H. Spurgeon said this about the genuineness of hope: "Hope itself is like a star—not to be seen in the sunshine of prosperity, and only to be discovered in the [dark] night of adversity." But please understand, there is one thing that Jesus cannot do for us, and that is to consciously choose Him, to commit our ways to Him and trust Him! And whether you are a believer in Christ or not, we all live in the same fallen world where suffering takes no prisoners. Pain sees no racial, religious, or political boundaries, and one out of every one people will someday die. The question is, where do you want to spend your eternity? You have the power to determine your own destiny.

"Dear Gracious, Faithful Savior, and Wonderful Redeemer, Lord, You have given us Your word and our hope in You is sure. "Truly, truly, You said to us, whoever believes in Me will also do the works that I do; and greater works than these will he do, because I am going to the Father. Whatever you ask in My name, this I will do, that the Father may be glorified in the Son. If you ask Me anything in my name, I will do it" (John 14:12–14, ESV).

Lord, Jesus, I pray for all those who read this account for the hope that is in me. That You will comfort those who are storm tossed in this life with no rest or comfort. Lord, cover them in Your mercy and grace, and fill them with your peace and then heal the broken-hearted and bind up their countless wounds. We live in an age when spiritual deception combined with a watered-down gospel has lured many good men, women, and children away from the pure milk of Your Word and truth. Instead of coming to the rock of our salvation and drinking from the fountain of life where hope, healing, and restoration is found, many have rejected Your counsel, while others are compromising the faith, becoming inebriated by drinking from the broken cisterns and poisoned waters of this intoxicating world, and—sadly, Lord—too many of those lives are ending in tragedy.

Help us to fix our hearts and eyes on Heaven above, to walk as You walked, desire what You desire, and do those things that You have always done. Fill us with Your truth and write these words on the tablets of our hearts that they might sustain us when our hearts are hurting and our spirits are broke. "Blessed are you who are poor, for yours is the kingdom of God. Blessed are you who are hungry now, for you shall be satisfied. Blessed are you who weep now, for you shall laugh. Blessed are you when people hate you and when they exclude you and revile you and spurn your name as evil, on account of the Son of Man! Rejoice in that day, and leap for joy, for behold, your reward is great in heaven" (Luke 6:20–23, ESV). Give us all, I pray, the grace, strength, love, and courage through Your Spirit and written Word to repent and return, then never retreat, or lose heart when doing good, knowing that in do season we will reap the reward if we don't lose heart.

Thank You, Lord Jesus, for, "Yours, O Lord, is the greatness and the power and the glory and the victory and the majesty, indeed everything that is in the heavens and the earth; Yours is the dominion, O Lord, and You exalt Yourself as head over all" (1 Chron. 29:11). I pray this today in Your mighty name, Jesus. Amen!

CHAPTER 1

THE UNKNOWN GOD

Most of us are familiar with the timeless adage, "If someone would have told me, I still wouldn't have believed them." Well, in my case, someone did tell me. Numerous times, in fact. And my response, sadly, was always the same: "That could never happen to someone like me!" But my mother wasn't the sort of woman who gave up easily. Mary Jeanette Lucas devoted her life to praying for me, and no matter how bleak things looked, she would often say, "Ellis, God told me you're going to be a preacher someday. God has great plans for your life." While she was nothing but confident, I couldn't imagine any scenario where that could ever happen. I was the youngest of four children and the only son, and my mom had particularly high hopes for my life—not to mention she loved Jesus more than anything, and nothing would have pleased her more than for me to make her dreams come true and become a preacher. Trouble is, there were a few obstacles that plagued my early life that, in my estimation, would be impossible to overcome.

I spent most of my adolescent and young adult years enslaved to numerous demonic strongholds, including years of drug and alcohol addiction, along with a volatile cocktail of anger, bitterness, hatred, violence, depression, etc. Additionally, I hated going to church, and the last thing I thought I would ever want to be was a preacher! Still, I would one day learn that nothing would frustrate the plans God had for my life, including my own unbelief and resistance! Sadly, my mom never lived to see her prediction come true. But her hopeful and encouraging words were fulfilled just as she'd predicted, and now there are absolutely no words in our English language adequate enough to describe the joy that God has filled my life with since that unforgettable day when Jesus Christ came into my life. Oh, what a day it was: March 6, 1997—the day my life became unshackled, and death, for me, was swallowed up in victory for good. It was my first day as Ellis Lucas, the born-again Christian, set apart by my Savior, transformed, and empowered for this purpose, that I may, as my precious mother predicted, proclaim the praises of Him Who called me out of darkness and into His marvelous light (1 Pet. 2:9).

Writing has surprisingly become an amazing yet totally unexpected outlet for proclaiming the unending praises of Jesus Christ. I say "surprisingly" because, after releasing *The Potter and the Clay* in early 2014, I never considered or felt the need to write a second book. But then again, I'd never planned to write a first book, so maybe the second shouldn't have surprised me. If anything, writing this book is yet another reminder of how God truly does work in mysterious and vastly unsearchable ways. Underscoring the total unlikelihood that I, Ellis Lucas, would write a book, you should know that I never studied literature, English, journalism, or anything of the sort. Truth is, I don't recall taking a single book home with me in all the years I attended school. I had never written anything of substantial length before, nor did I have any way of knowing that my story would one day pull on the heartstrings of numerous other broken lives in need of hope, healing, and restoration. Both my books and the songs I have written and recorded were, for all intents and purposes, strictly spontaneous, emphasizing yet again how God surprises us.

It brings to mind 1 Corinthians 2:9: "Eye has not seen, nor ear heard, nor have entered into the heart of man the things which God has prepared for those who love Him!" Be that as it may, until March 6, 1997—and despite the fact that I was raised in church and was the son of a mother whose life portrayed the Gospel—Jesus Christ was still a distant, faraway stranger to me. I had grown up hearing all about Him, but nevertheless, I didn't know Him. John 1:10 which says, "He was in the world, and the world was made through Him, yet the world did not know Him" (John 1:10, ESV), could have just as easily been written about our generation in that, much of society today, doesn't have a personal relationship with Him, in a similar way that only a small number of people of His day did. It wasn't that most of the people—including and the religious community—had not heard of Jesus, because they had. In fact, once Jesus took center stage doing those things that no one else had ever done before, such as the blind receiving their sight, the lame walking, the lepers being cleansed, the deaf hearing, and the dead being brought back to life after as much as four days in the grave, He was more than likely the most famous man on earth (Matt. 11:5)!

The problem, however, was that He came to His own, and those who were His own did not receive Him (John 1:11). The people that did know who Jesus was had a hard time accepting Jesus's claim to deity, as in John chapter six, or that He had come down from heaven. And in their defense, it would be shocking to hear someone we had grown up with and knew of their family claim to be the Creator of the universe. Nevertheless, they were responsible for knowing signs of the time and of the coming of the promised Messiah. But unfortunately they were saying, "We've known Him all His life, and even His parents. How can He say that He came down from heaven?" They, in fact, had a point in saying they had known Jesus and His family all His life. However, they were not there when the angel Gabriel came to Mary, and they were not there when Mary, expecting Jesus, visited Elizabeth, who at the time was expecting John the Baptist. Nor were they there when the Spirit in John the Baptist, who was still in Elizabeth's womb, leaped when He recognized Jesus in the womb of Mary. No, and furthermore, no flesh and blood was there when the Bridal Price (Mohar) was agreed upon. Nor were they there when the angels appeared to the shepherds, saying, "Unto you is born this day in the city of David a Savior," or when the Voice from heaven said, "This is My Beloved Son, in Whom I am well pleased." There are other references, but the point is that these people, though they knew many facts about Jesus—just as I did and many of you also do—they did not know or understand who Jesus is or have a personal relationship with Him.

Paul, standing in the midst of the Areopagus (the hill of Mars, which was the seat of the ancient and esteemed supreme court of Athens, called the Areopagites), said,

> Men of Athens, I perceive that in every way you are very religious. For as I passed along and observed the objects of your worship, I found also an altar with this inscription: "To the unknown god." What therefore you worship as unknown, this I proclaim to you. The God Who made the world and everything in it, being Lord of heaven and earth, does not live in temples made by man, nor is He served by human hands, as though He needed anything, since He Himself gives to all mankind life and breath and everything. And He made from one man every nation of mankind to live on all the face of the earth, having determined allotted periods and the boundaries of their dwelling place, that they should seek God, and perhaps feel their way toward Him and find Him. Yet He is actually not far from each one of us, for "In Him we live and move and have our being"; as even some of your own poets have said, "For we are indeed His offspring!" (Acts 17:22–28)

Much of America, along with much of the population that makes up western civilization today, has a similar view of Jesus as the people of His time. Furthermore, Jesus told His disciples the world hated Him because He testified of it, that its deeds are evil. "And this is the condemnation," said the Apostle John, "that Light is come into the world, and men loved darkness rather than light, because their deeds were evil" (John 3:19). The postmodernist would argue that Jesus is only one of many ways to heaven—that Jesus is the Way, Truth, and Life for Christians only. But Jesus Himself cried out to God the Father, pleading, "Father, if there is any other way, please take this cup of suffering from Me. But nevertheless, not My will, but Thy will be done" (Matt. 26:39). Soon thereafter he was beaten beyond recognition and crucified, signifying that He is the narrow gate that opens unto salvation for reconciliation for the broken and bruised members of this present age, to find hope and healing when in fact, nothing else can transform and restore a shattered life!

All four gospels and Tacitus in Annals (XV, 44) agree that the crucifixion occurred when Pontius Pilate was procurator of Judea from 26 to 36 AD. All four gospels say the crucifixion occurred on a Friday. All four gospels agree that Jesus died a few hours before the beginning of the Jewish Sabbath (nightfall on a Friday). The Gospel of Matthew says,

> And Jesus cried out again with a loud voice, and yielded up His spirit. And behold, the veil of the temple was torn in two from top to bottom; and the earth shook and the rocks were split. The tombs were opened, and many bodies of the saints who had fallen asleep were raised; and coming out of the tombs after His resurrection they entered the holy city and appeared to many. Now the centurion, and those who were with him keeping guard over Jesus, when they saw the earthquake and the things that were happening, became very frightened and said, "Truly this was the Son of God." (Matt. 27:50–54, NASB)

In an NBC News report by Jennifer Viegas (May 24, 2012), geologists say Jesus, as described in the New Testament, was most likely crucified on Friday, April 3, in the year 33 AD. The latest investigation, reported in *International Geology Review*, focused on earthquake activity at the Dead Sea, located thirteen miles from Jerusalem. The Gospel of Matthew, Chapter 27, mentions that an earthquake coincided with the crucifixion:

> To analyze earthquake activity in the region, geologist Jefferson Williams of Supersonic Geophysical and colleagues Markus Schwab and

Achim Brauer of the German Research Center for Geosciences studied three cores from the beach of the Ein Gedi Spa adjacent to the Dead Sea. Varves, which are annual layers of deposition in the sediments, reveal that at least two major earthquakes affected the core: a widespread earthquake in 31 B.C. and a seismic event that happened sometime between the years 26 A.D. and 36 A.D. The latter period occurred during "the years when Pontius Pilate was procurator of Judea and when the earthquake of the Gospel of Matthew is historically constrained," Williams said. "The day and date of the crucifixion (Good Friday) are known with a fair degree of precision," he said. But the year has been in question.

The Gospel, meaning Good News according to John, says,

> In the beginning was the Word, and the Word was with God, and the Word was God. He was in the beginning with God. All things were made through Him, and without Him nothing was made that was made. In Him was life, and the life was the light of men. And the light shines in the darkness, and the darkness did not comprehend it. (John 1:1–5, NKJV)

One of the evidences used in defending the deity of the Christ is the testimony of prophecy. There are numerous Messianic prophecies regarding Jesus Christ in the Old Testament. Prophecies that were made centuries before the birth of Jesus Christ that were very specific in detail. Skeptics have questioned the date of these prophecies and even charged that they were not recorded until after or during the time of Jesus, therefore discounted their prophetic nature. However, one of the most important discoveries of the modern era is the Dead Sea scrolls which contained a complete copy of the Isaiah

Scroll, the book of Isaiah. This twenty-four-foot-long scroll is well preserved and dates to between 100 BC and 300 BC. It contains one of the clearest and most detailed prophecies of the Messiah recorded in chapter fifty-three, called the "Suffering Servant." This prophecy can only refer to Jesus Christ and here are just a few reasons. The suffering servant is called sinless (53:9), he dies and rises from the dead (53:8–10), and he suffers and dies for the sins of the people (53:4–6). The Isaiah Scroll gives us a manuscript that predates the birth of Christ by a minimum, over a century and contains many of the most important messianic prophecies about Jesus in the entire Old Testament. Skeptics could no longer contend that portions of the book were written after Christ or that first century insertions were added to the text. The Dead Sea Scrolls provide additional proof that the Old Testament canon was completed by the third century BC, and that the prophecies foretold of Christ in the Old Testament predated the birth of Christ.

Peter Flint, a graduate student who moved from South Africa to the United States and attended the University of Notre Dame and helped publish the Dead Sea Scrolls, said, "The Dead Sea Scrolls are the greatest find of our time. They affect our understanding of the Bible and they confirm the accuracy of Scripture. They enhance our understanding of Jesus and help us interpret the New Testament." Again, Paul said the gospel is more than just good news saying, "I am not ashamed of the gospel, for it is the power of God for salvation to everyone who believes, to the Jew first and also to the Greek" (Rom. 1:16, ESV)!

When my life was suddenly taken from my control and in an instant appeared to be over while staying at a drug house in Gladstone, Missouri—the morning when the Kansas City SWAT team raided the house, and we were all arrested and charged on felony drug charges that carried a fifteen-year-to-life sentence if convicted—there was only one Who extended His mercy and grace to me that day, and His name is Jesus! My life was completely transformed from a hopeless impaired addict to Ellis Lucas, healed and in my right mind all in a day. I echo Paul's declaration to Timothy where he said,

> I thank Him Who has given me strength, Christ Jesus our Lord, because He judged me faithful, appointing me to His service, though formerly I was a blasphemer, persecutor, and insolent opponent. But I received mercy because I had acted ignorantly in unbelief, and the grace of our Lord overflowed for me with the faith and love that are in Christ Jesus. The saying is trustworthy and deserving of full acceptance, that Christ Jesus came into the world to save sinners, of whom I am the foremost. But mercy was given to me for this reason, that in me, as the foremost, Jesus Christ might display His perfect patience as an example to those who were to believe in Him for eternal life. To the King of the ages, immortal, invisible, the only God, be honor and glory forever and ever. Amen. (1 Tim. 1:12–17)

For several years, our organization collaborated with a lady named Karen Hulbert, who founded and ran an equine (horse) therapy outreach ministry for women. Most of the women in the program were former prison inmates desperately trying to reacclimate back into society. Some had been emotionally and/or physically abused, and the scars they bore on both their hearts and bodies made it nearly impossible for some of those ladies to even communicate with other people before entering Karen's program. Yet amazingly, in just over five years of working together, I was—and still am today—astonished that only one girl that I know of during that time returned to jail. That is simply a remarkable percentage, especially when nearly two-thirds (sixty-eight percent) of 405,000 prisoners released in thirty states in 2005 were arrested for a new crime within three years of release from prison, and three-quarters (seventy-seven percent) were arrested within five years, per the Bureau of Justice Statistics (BJS).

What is the secret to her success, you might ask? Well, there is no secret to what she does. What Karen offers these girls has been readily available since the dawn of creation: faith, hope, and love—the three liberating characteristics that come from knowing the Way, the Truth, and the Life! Karen knows that the same indescribable, incomprehensible Jesus Who numbers the stars and calls them all by name is the same Jesus Who healed her former broken heart and bound up her own wounds (Ps. 147:3–4). What's more, it is the same Jesus Who put back the pieces of my former shattered life and restored the heartbreaking years lost to sin and the destructiveness of my own deceitful heart!

Faith is grounded in truth, because without knowing the truth it would be impossible to have real faith. Faith comes by hearing, and hearing by the Word of God (Rom. 10:17). That's why Jesus said to the Jews who had believed Him, "If you abide in My word, you are truly My disciples, and you will know the truth, and the truth will set you free" (John 8:31–32). So, if you have faith and have been liberated through the Word of God, you will never again be without genuine hope. Why? Because "faith is the *substance* of things *hoped* for, the *evidence* of things not seen" (Heb. 11:1, emphasis added).

Fear, on the other hand, is the exact opposite of faith. Simply stated, fear can be defined as unbelief. As unbelief gains the upper hand in our thoughts, fear takes hold of our emotions. Our deliverance from fear and worry is dependent on faith, which is the opposite of unbelief. We also need to understand that faith is not something that we can produce in ourselves. Faith is a gift (Eph. 2:8–9) and is described as a fruit (or characteristic) which is produced in our lives by the Holy Spirit (Gal. 5:22). As Christians, our faith is a confident assurance in a God Who loves us, Who knows our thoughts and cares about our deepest needs—a God Who is our ever-present, all-sufficient help in time of need (Ps. 46:1) but is also a Father Who disciplines His children, authenticating the genuineness of your adoption and acceptance as a child who is loved and nurtured by God (Heb. 12)! Those who attain a genuine faith—the substance of things hoped for—also, though unseen, produce the evidence that they have attained and encountered genuine Christian love. In other words, God's perfect love casts out all fear (1 John 4:18).

Life is full of exciting peaks and deep painful valleys, and our hearts were made to break. But we can count on these comforts: God is not a man; He will not lie. God is not a human being; His decisions will not change. If He says He will do something, then He will do it. If He makes a promise, then He will do what He promised (Num. 23:19).

Paul said, "Do not be conformed to this world, but be transformed by the renewing of your mind, that you may *prove* what is that good and acceptable and perfect will of God" (Rom. 12:2, emphasis added)! That verse alone holds the key to unlocking the full potential to who and what we were all created to be! How do we prove something in a court of law? By presenting hard, indisputable evidence. So again, what is faith? The *evidence* of things not yet seen. We are transformed by the washing of water by the Word of God (Rom. 5:8), and not because of works done by us in righteousness, but according to his own mercy, by the washing of regeneration and renewal of the Holy Spirit (Tit. 3:5, ESV).

> Blessed is the man who walks not in the counsel of the ungodly, nor stands in the path of sinners, nor sits in the seat of the scornful; but his delight is in the law [word] of the Lord, and in His law [word] he meditates day and night. He shall be like a tree planted by the rivers of water, that brings forth its fruit in its season, whose leaf also shall not wither; and whatever he does shall prosper. (Ps. 1:1–3)

However, when the Word of God says to forgive as we also have been forgiven, it doesn't necessarily mean the person that hurt you deserves your mercy, because the truth is, none of us do. But just as Woodrow Kroll once said, "Justice is for those who deserve it; mercy is for those who don't." So, post this passage on the doorpost of your heart and mind and practice them, which says,

> Do not fret because of evildoers, nor be envious of the workers of iniquity. For they shall soon be cut down like the grass, and wither as the green herb. But instead, trust in the Lord, and do good; dwell in the land, and feed on His faithfulness. Delight yourself also in the Lord, and He shall give you the desires of your heart. Commit your way to the Lord, trust also in Him, and He shall bring it to pass. (Ps. 37:1–5)

The secret to the great success of the women's outreach ministry mentioned earlier lies in the hands Karen Hulbert, a modern-day version of both "Lois" and "Eunice," the grandmother and mother (respectively) of Timothy, Paul's young disciple that was so gifted in the Word. These two women had raised Timothy not only in the faith but also in the study of the Sacred Writings (the inspired Word of God). It was this early study of Sacred Letters, carried on in the home, that helped set this young man's soul on fire, ground him in his faith, and fall in love with Jesus Christ. Karen, much like Lois and Eunice, has loved the women impacted by her ministry as if they were her very own children—a love that they had either never experienced or had long forgotten its power! She accepted them just as they were, and with God's help, she not only taught them who they are in Christ but also, in the process, wrote the Word of God on the tablets of their hearts. And not only has time and these precious ladies' lives proved that they know Who Jesus Christ is, but they also know and love Him deeply, and just like Mary and Martha, they now each enjoy a very personal and meaningful relationship with Him, and credit Him for being the one Who healed their broken hearts and bound up their many wounds!

In writing this book, I hope to expose the lies of Satan regarding God's infinite love toward you, regardless of your past or present situation. For example, consider the Lord's own words spoken to and through the young prophet Jeremiah:

> "For I know the plans I have for you," declares the Lord, "plans to prosper you and not to harm you, plans to give you hope and a future. Then you will call on Me and come and pray to Me, and I will listen to you. You will seek Me and find Me when you seek Me with all your heart. I will be found by you," declares the Lord, "and will bring you back from captivity." (Jer. 29:11–14)

In Psalm 139, David said,

> You formed my inward parts; You covered me in my mother's womb. I will praise You, for I am fearfully and wonderfully made; marvelous are Your works, and that my soul knows very well. My frame was not hidden from You, when I was made in secret, and skillfully wrought in the lowest parts of the earth. Your eyes saw my substance, being yet unformed. And in Your book they all were written, the days fashioned for me, when as yet there were none of them. How precious also are Your thoughts to me, O God! How great is the sum of them! If I should count them, they would be more in number than the sand; when I awake, I am still with You. (Ps. 139:13–18)

Perhaps you're wrestling with doubt, fear, and are riddled with anxiety, teetering on the brink of giving up in despair and losing hope. Well, be of good cheer, because no matter how far hope, revival, or victory may seem removed from our generation, salvation, hope, change—and, yes, even total renewal—are never out of reach with Jesus. If you search for Him with all your heart, he will be found and be abundantly made known to you.

> May He grant you according to the riches of His glory, strength coupled with might through His Spirit in the inner man that Christ may dwell in your heart through faith. That you, being rooted and grounded in love, may be able to comprehend with all the saints what is the width and length and depth and height—to know the love of Christ which passes knowledge; that you may be filled with all the fullness of God. And finally, to Him alone who is able to do exceedingly abundantly above all that we ask or think, according to the power that works in us, to Him be glory in the church by Christ Jesus to all generations, both now and forever and ever more. (Eph. 3:16–21, NASB)

Amen!

CHAPTER 2

GOD'S MOST WANTED

In Mark chapter five, we find a heart-wrenching story of a tormented man living in total isolation, demon possessed, and suffering the consequences of a life separated from God by sin. Night and day, the Bible says, he could be heard crying out near the empty tombs (a place synonymous with death, disease, suffering, and decay) and on the mountaintops, cutting himself with sharp, jagged stones (a very graphic portrait of an extremely desperate and heavily burdened man)!

While the Bible doesn't explain—nor does it need to explain—what happened during this man's life that opened the door for the horrific condition he was in at the time of his encounter with Jesus Christ, something obviously went awry to cause this tragic outcome. But what a blessing it is in knowing how much our Lord cares about our joy and peace of mind, going to great lengths to assure us that none of our past mistakes are relevant to Him once we have trusted Him as both Lord and Savior. Furthermore, He reveals that no one is beyond His ability to forgive, heal, and restore, demonstrating that "as far as the east is from the west, so far has He removed our transgressions from us" (Ps. 103:12).

We've all done things we're not proud of and have made mistakes we wish we could erase. I believe this story, like my own, was recorded for one purpose: to shine the light on Jesus Christ and the power of His redeeming love! Mark 5:19 supports that thought, with Jesus saying, "Go home to your friends and tell them how much the

40

Lord has done for you, and how He has had mercy on you." This story has less to do with the demoniac and everything to do with you and me today knowing God and making Him known to our generation. In addition, it proves that God shows no partiality toward any people (Acts 10:34)! God is not a respecter of persons. He does not show partiality or favoritism, and neither should we. When we believe in God, He promises to give us a new heart and put a new spirit within us, regardless of what condition we may be in, thereby removing the heart of stone from within us and creating a new heart of flesh (Ezek. 36:26)!

The truth is, prior to us being born again and made alive in Jesus Christ, we were all just as impoverished of life as the demoniac. Ephesians chapter two says that by grace Christians are made alive, who were dead in trespasses and sins, in which we all once walked according to the course of this world, according to the prince of the power of the air (Satan), the spirit who now works in the sons of disobedience, among whom also we all once conducted ourselves in the lusts of our flesh, fulfilling the desires of the flesh and of the mind, and were by nature children of wrath, just as the others (Eph. 2:1–3).

One thing we can all agree on is this: that dead people can't do anything for themselves; simply put, they're dead. On the other hand, the Gospel, which is anchored to the hope of life eternal through the finished work of Jesus Christ on the cross, abolishes the penalty for sin and removes the sting of death altogether for all people who have placed their hope in Jesus Christ. Jesus said, "I am the resurrection and the life. He who believes in Me, though he may die, he shall live. And whoever lives and believes in Me shall never die. Do you believe this?" (John 11:25–26).

There are countless wounded souls feeling abandoned, rejected, unloved, unwanted, and, in many cases, damaged beyond hope! If that sounds like you, I want you to know that you're not hopeless! Satan not only understands all too well how the truth will make you free, but he is also terrified of you learning the truth about your true purpose in this life. I did, and my advice to you is this: don't give up; Satan's words are all a big lie! God is a Father to the fatherless and a judge for the widows. God makes a home for the lonely, and He leads the prisoners out of bondage and into prosperity (Ps. 68:5).

Whenever I read the story of the demoniac, I am always astonished at the differences between what God thought of that man as opposed to the people's perspective. The community undoubtedly ostracized him, and rather by choice or by some type of order, he was found living among the tombs when Jesus Christ crossed the Sea of Galilee and changed his life forever. Luke 8:27b says, "For a long time he had worn no clothes, and he had not lived in a house but among the tombs." Luke 8:29 adds, "He was kept under guard and bound with chains and shackles, but he would break the bonds and be driven by the demon into the desert." But when the demoniac saw Jesus from afar, he ran and fell down before Him. Then, crying out with a loud voice, he said, "What have You to do with me, Jesus, Son of the Most High God? I adjure You by God, do not torment me," for Jesus was saying to him, "Come out of the man, you unclean spirit."

In my Bible dictionary, the word *adjure* is defined this way: "To command solemnly under or as if under oath or penalty of a curse. Or to request or advise solemnly." Whatever the reason for this strange request, these fallen angels both know and dreadfully fear the coming consequences associated with their failed attempt at overthrowing God's unshakable kingdom (Heb. 12:28). "'Upon this rock I will build My church,' Said the Lord, 'And the gates of Hades shall not prevail against it'" (Matt. 16:18)! The truth is, however, Satan will try, but his only weapon of warfare against humanity is psychological warfare—a near carbon copy of what we see in Genesis chapter three, which took place just prior to the fall.

> Now the serpent [Satan] who was more crafty than any other beast of the field that the Lord God had made said to the woman, "Did God actually say, 'You shall not eat of any tree in the garden'?" And the woman said to the serpent, "We may eat of the fruit of the trees in the garden, but God said, 'You shall not eat of the

fruit of the tree that is in the midst of the garden, neither shall you touch it, lest you die.'" But the serpent said to the woman, "You will not surely die. For God knows that when you eat of it your eyes will be opened, and you will be like God, knowing good and evil." So when the woman saw that the tree was good for food, and that it was a delight to the eyes, and that the tree was to be desired to make one wise, she took of its fruit and ate, and she also gave some to her husband who was with her, and he ate. (Gen. 3:1–6)

And just like it was in the garden (read Genesis 3:14–15), we see the uncontested power and authority of Jesus as He confronts these merciless agents of Satan, asking, "What is your name?" The demoniac replied, "My name is Legion, for we are many." And he begged the Lord earnestly not to send them out of the country.

I know from experience that if there's one thing that strikes fear in the darkened soul of Satan, it's the name of Jesus! Furthermore, not even this army of demons would dare challenge the power and authority of Jesus Christ! Instead, upon seeing a great herd of pigs feeding on a hillside nearby, they begged Jesus, saying, "Send us to the pigs; let us enter them." The unclean spirits came out of this suffering man and entered the pigs, and the herd, numbering about two thousand, rushed down the steep bank into the sea and drowned. The herdsmen then fled and told those in the city and in the country about the occurrence. And the people came to see what it was that had happened. And the multitudes came to Jesus and saw the demon-possessed man—the one who'd had the legion—sitting there, clothed, at peace, and in his right mind, and they were afraid.

When Jesus Christ transformed my life in March of 1997, it startled many people. A personal encounter with the Creator of the universe isn't the sort of thing our finite understandings—including my own—is accustomed to dealing with, and when it does happen, it has a very sobering effect on everyone! Likewise, the people who were present and witnessed the Mark 5 account described what had happened to the demon-possessed man and to the pigs. And the people began to beg Jesus to depart from their region. Jesus humbly honored their requests, even as He still does for those in our lifetime who reject His mercy and blessing intended for their lives. But this former demon-possessed man did no such thing. Instead, as Jesus was getting into the boat, he begged our Lord Jesus that he might be with Him. However, He did not permit him but said to him, "'Go home to your friends and tell them how much the Lord has done for you, and how He has had mercy on you.' And he went away and began to proclaim in the Decapolis how much Jesus had done for him, and everyone marveled" (Mark 5:2–20)!

If you read *The Potter and the Clay* then you may remember how, when I was wrestling with going back to my hometown in Stanberry, Missouri, along with a few other friends I grew up with that had since become Christians, it wasn't until the subject of us ministering to our old friends came up that I had peace about going. And had it not been for that step of faith, there may not be a His Heart United Ministries. Perhaps that is why the Lord instructed the demoniac to go home to his friends and share what great things God had done for him. I don't know, but what the Bible does say is that the people who were present when the Lord arrived with His disciples and healed him were undoubtedly terrified yet remained unrepentant. Their natural reaction was that they wanted nothing more to do with Jesus. This not only reveals the hardness of their hearts but also, quite honestly, represents an even more revealing truth regarding how the economic effects of losing a couple of thousand pigs was far more important to them than this formerly tormented man being healed and restored back to good health and a sound mind.

Unfortunately, things haven't changed much since Jesus's day. And even though the Mark 5 event took place some two thousand years ago, the story has never been more relevant or needed than it is right here and now in our lifetime. But also notice that with Jesus, it was—and still is—exactly the opposite. Today's postmodern society has devalued life to the point of seeing certain individuals' lives as nothing more than a hopeless liability and, quite frankly, disposable. Jesus, on the other hand, demonstrated His heart and set a very powerful, contrasting standard here just as He had done when He healed the blind beggar. However, if being blind wasn't bad enough, unfortunately, being healed by the Lord created a whole new array of problems as the religious leaders immediately began to revile him, saying,

> "You are His [Jesus] disciple, but we are disciples of Moses. We know that God has spoken to Moses, but as for this man, we do not know where He comes from." The [former blind] man answered, "Why, this is an amazing thing! You do not know where He comes from, and yet He opened my eyes. We know that God does not listen to sinners, but if anyone is a worshiper of God and does His will, God listens to him. Never since the world began has it been heard that anyone opened the eyes of a man born blind. If this man were not from God, He could do nothing." They answered Him, "You were born in utter sin, and would You teach us?" And they cast Him out. (John 9:28–34)

It was a common belief in Jewish culture that tragedy and suffering were a direct result of some great sin, and, unfortunately, the religious leaders and their followers believed this man was blind because of sin, and no one felt compelled to help him. Be that as it may, it is very easy for any of us to see a need in someone's life and not do anything about it. We can look at someone's needs and think they are in that situation because of some sin or bad judgment. And don't get me wrong—sin will always result in consequences. And yes, this is a tragedy. But an even greater tragedy is the veil of blindness over the minds and hearts of unbelievers which prevents them from seeing the light of the gospel of Jesus (2 Cor. 4:4–6).

In any case, excuses help us avoid responsibility when it comes to helping others. Jesus, on the other hand, looked at the blind man, saw his need, and unapologetically met it. Remember what Jesus said in Matthew 25 as a warning to those who neglect the downcast. He said there would come a day when, after His return to planet Earth, there would be a literal separation of the believers (His sheep) from the nonbelievers (Satan's goats), and to the nonbelievers He will say,

> "Depart from Me, you cursed, into the everlasting fire prepared for the devil and his angels: for I was hungry and you gave Me no food; I was thirsty and you gave Me no drink; I was a stranger and you did not take Me in, naked and you did not clothe Me, sick and in prison and you did not visit Me." Then they also will answer Him, saying, "Lord, when did we see You hungry or thirsty or a stranger or naked or sick or in prison, and did not minister to You?" Then He will answer them, saying, "Assuredly, I say to you, inasmuch as you did not do it to one of the least of these, you did not do it to Me." And these will go away into everlasting punishment, but the righteous into eternal life. (Matt. 25:41–46)

Don't be deceived, friends. God is not mocked; for whatever a man sows, that he will also reap. For he who sows to his flesh will of the flesh reap corruption, but he who sows to the Spirit will of the Spirit reap everlasting life (Gal. 6:7–8). Furthermore, watch over your heart with all diligence, for from it flow the wellsprings of life (Prov. 4:20–23)! God's heart breaks for the lonely, He grieves for the lowly, and He defends the fatherless, the abandoned, and the broken. He heals the brokenhearted and binds up their wounds (Ps. 147:3) and says, "Blessed are the poor in spirit, for theirs is the kingdom of heaven. Blessed are those who mourn, for they shall be comforted" (Matt. 5:3–4)!

The healed and now former demoniac, on the other hand, demonstrated a genuine mountain-moving faith combined with genuine biblical repentance that was validated by a changed heart as well as a healed and sound mind. "For God hath not given us the spirit of fear, but of power and of love and of a sound mind" (2 Tim. 1:7)!

God had plans for this man's life that would soon turn the entire region up on end. Furthermore, it's not hard to notice how the heart truly is deceitful above all things and desperately wicked. Who can know it? "But I, says the Lord, search the heart, and test the mind, even to give to every man according to his ways, according to the fruit of his doings" (Jer. 17:9–10)!

Moses, who was raised by Pharaoh's daughter, was well-educated and could have ruled all the nations of the world had that been his desire, and yet he refused to be called the son of Pharaoh's daughter. He chose not to enjoy the temporary, passing pleasures of sin that last only for a moment and instead chose to suffer with God's people, considering the reproach of the Lord to be greater riches than all the treasures of Egypt, for he was looking to the reward (Heb. 11:24–25).

Finally, I will wrap up this chapter with one of the greatest stories in the entire Bible of unjust suffering (though none can compare to the crucifixion of our Lord and Savior Jesus Christ)—the story of Joseph. Joseph, in many ways, represents a foreshadowing of the life of Jesus and a portrait of the Gospel. God had shown Joseph through various dreams and visions that he was a very special individual in some way. Joseph just didn't know at that time in *what* way. And when things began to rise against him, he must have wondered if he had misinterpreted God's plans for him.

His brothers sold him into slavery in Egypt. Potiphar's wife falsely accused him of trying to rape her, and, as a result, Joseph was thrown into prison. But it was there that God began to change his conditions. Because he had interpreted dreams for Pharaoh's servants in prison, he was also called on to interpret Pharaoh's dreams, and he prophesied that a famine would come in seven years. After Pharaoh saw that Joseph had unusual wisdom and insight, he put him in charge of all Egypt in preparation for the famine he had prophesied. Years later, by the time the famine had spread over the earth, Joseph had already built up large stores of grain in Egypt and had, for all intents and purposes, become the greatest human being on the planet. Whatever he wanted was his, and at that point Joseph had become untouchable.

When Jacob heard that there was food in Egypt, he sent his sons, Joseph's brothers, to Egypt to buy grain. They bought grain from Joseph, but they didn't recognize him, and he didn't tell them who he was during their first two visits. When he finally did reveal himself to his brothers, he told them to go back to Canaan and get their families, their father, and his full-blooded younger brother Benjamin, who was so near and dear to Joseph's heart as was his father Jacob. Joseph explained to them how even though he had been sold into slavery out of bad motives, God had planned it for good in order to save many people (Gen. 50:20). Looking back on his life, he could see that God had been working all things together for his good that entire time! His brothers went back to Canaan and brought their families, Benjamin, and Jacob to Egypt. Joseph provided a good land for them to live in. Joseph's life is a symbolic portrait of Jesus's life in many ways. Joseph was rejected by his brothers just as Jesus was rejected by His own (John 1:11–13). Then Joseph went to another region (Egypt) to prepare a place for his family, just as Jesus also said He was going to prepare a place for us in heaven (John 14:3). Joseph had a divine purpose just like you and I do. Jesus had a divine purpose—to give His life as a ransom for the many who would one day believe on His name!

Neither Joseph's nor Jesus's lives were easy, just as our lives are not easy. Although there were many seasons when Joseph must have wrestled with doubt and fear, wondering if God had abandoned him, just like John the Baptist—the greatest of all the men who ever lived, according to the Lord Himself—had done, as recorded in John chapter seven, which says,

> And John, calling two of his disciples to him, sent them to Jesus, saying, "Are You the Coming One, or do we look for another?" When the men had come to Him, they said, "John the Baptist has sent us to You, saying, 'Are You the Coming One, or do we look for another?'" And that very hour He cured many of infirmities, afflictions, and evil spirits; and to many blind

He gave sight. Jesus answered and said to them, "Go and tell John the things you have seen and heard: that the blind see, the lame walk, the lepers are cleansed, the deaf hear, the dead are raised, the poor have the gospel preached to them. And blessed is he who is not offended because of Me." (John 7:19–23)

The Lord, while speaking through the prophet Isaiah approximately 740 years prior to Him being born in Bethlehem, said this about the coming Messiah:

The Spirit of the Lord God is upon Me, because the Lord has anointed Me to preach good tidings to the poor; He has sent Me to heal the brokenhearted, to proclaim liberty to the captives, and the opening of the prison to those who are bound; to proclaim the acceptable year of the Lord, and the day of vengeance of our God; to comfort all who mourn, to console those who mourn in Zion, to give them beauty for ashes, the oil of joy for mourning, the garment of praise for the spirit of heaviness; that they may be called trees of righteousness, the planting of the Lord, that He may be glorified. (Isa. 61:1–3)

Joseph undoubtedly knew that there was so much more to life than what he could see and experience—and the same is true in this present dark age. He found favor with God by staying focused on God and His will instead of his own will or circumstances, always allowing God to use him wherever he went. The question is are you focused on Jesus Christ, or are you focused on your circumstances or the situation in which you may currently find yourself? Another point in my writing this book is to testify of those great things that I have experienced that were all recorded in the Bible, the immutable promises of God to encourage you to know and believe that God not only loves you more than life itself, but also that He is challenging you to take that life-changing step of faith with your life as I did with mine, saying, "Call unto Me, and I will answer thee, and show thee great and mighty things, which you do not know" (Jer. 33:3)! Amen!

CHAPTER 3

ALL THAT IS IN THE WORLD

Likewise, all that is in the world—the lust of the flesh, the lust of the eyes, and the pride of life—are the three most seductive temptations that Satan has used to ravage families, leaving many innocent lives crushed, confused, and quite literally devastated, especially when sacred vows have been violated or someone has been betrayed by someone they love. These are most certainly not of the Father but are of the world, in which Satan is referred to in the Bible as the god of this world. We all struggle with pride in life! Sadly, though, many of us do so because we do not realize the potential that waits for us if we will just humble ourselves beneath the mighty hand of God, let go of all we are holding onto, and move forward in God's plans for our lives.

Pride is often a mechanism we use to cover up the reality that we don't want others to know about us—our fears, our insecurities, and our innumerable flaws. Remarkably, society has now become so obsessed with outward beauty and appearance that, according to the Cosmetic Surgery National Data Bank Statistics, in just one year (2016), Americans alone spent more than fifteen billion dollars on combined surgical and nonsurgical procedures for the first time ever on a quest to be the person they think is going to make them more confident, attractive etc.—the very things that got Satan cast out of heaven and condemned to an eternal conscious existence in a burning lake of fire. Hell is a place described as total darkness in a lake of fire that burns forever without end with no hope for acquittal or absolution and where the torment never ends. What happened, you might ask? The conception of lust and pride. God reprimanded Satan by saying, "Your heart was proud because of your beauty; you corrupted your wisdom for the sake of your splendor. I cast you to the ground; I exposed you before kings, to feast their eyes on you" (Ezek. 28:17).

These were stats released by The American Society for Aesthetic Plastic Surgery. If only people could see themselves through the eyes of God, who calls us His workmanship (*poiéma*, pronounced poy'-ay-mah) created in Christ Jesus for a far more, exceedingly, abundantly above-and-beyond purpose (Eph. 2:10–3:20), then they would see their magnificent beauty, priceless value, and endless potential waiting to behold the moment they finally realize they were fearfully, wonderfully, and gloriously made from the beginning. For instance, the Bible says a virtuous wife is worth more than all the precious stones in the world (Prov. 31:10). What could possibly be more desired or beautiful than all the priceless stones in the world? A virtuous woman!

When I first met my wife Peggi, there was something so bright and beautiful about her that, figuratively speaking, it took my breath away—a beauty so stunning it was like looking at a precious stone so transparent and pure that I couldn't take my eyes off of her for a second. And when the Lord said, "Ellis, that's the woman you're going to marry," I could hardly breathe. I stood frozen in place, speechless and momentarily paralyzed with fear, wondering what a girl like that could possibly want or need with someone like me. And over time, as our friendship began to mature, I was shocked to discover how her unmistakable beauty was forged out of a deep and painful life, beginning with a dark cloud of crippling depression that she somehow managed to endure during her adolescent years followed by years of insecurities and inner conflicts that only served to intensify her poor self-image. Not surprisingly, her parents had divorced when she was young, and she was reared in a single-parent home where many men had come and gone. Later in life she found herself trying to be a great and loving mother to her two kids after losing the father of her children and her only husband, who had died at age thirty-eight to a fatal heart attack.

Were there moments of doubt and fear? Was there ever a thought or temptation to give in and take her own life? Of course! But *Jesus*! And just as He said to me on March 6, 1997— "Ellis, I love you, and I'm here for you. I know your situation, and yes, I am concerned for you! But, Ellis, I have a plan for your life, and I can help. If you will put your trust in Me today, everything is going to be just fine!"—He, too, said to her, "I know the plans I have for you. Plans for good and not for evil, to give you a future and a hope! Peggi, if you will just trust in Me today, I give you My word that everything is going to be just fine!" Amen! Her love for Jesus was so real and powerful that it became the catalyst for the rapid rise of His Heart United Ministries along with a contagious love that affects nearly everyone she comes into contact with through her profession as a family nurse practitioner and the ministry God has raised up through this unlikely union that has now become the strength and love of both our lives!

Peggi is that virtuous woman spoken of in Proverbs 31:10, a very rare and priceless jewel formed and polished over the course of a lifetime like a precious pearl—a process that is accomplished through much suffering. Suffering is a way of perfection, even for Christians. Like the slow-forming pearl, it is hidden from the world, like the mystery of the Gospel. Also, a pearl is incapable of freeing itself. It is clamped tight within the structure of the clam in a similar way that so many bounded souls are imprisoned to drug and alcohol addictions, anger, pornography, fear and paranoia, or bitterness toward others who have ruthlessly trespassed against them. The same is true for them. It will only be freed when it is found by someone in search of whatever is inside the shell. But if the Son sets you free, you're free indeed (John 8:36)! Peggi in Hebrew means "pearl."

God said, "I will search for the lost and bring back the strays. I will bind up the injured and strengthen the weak, but the sleek and the strong I will destroy. I will shepherd the flock with justice" (Ezek. 34:16)! The true value of the pearl is not seen from the outside. To the world around it, the pearl is just another appendage covered by a nasty hard outer shell. The Lord looks upon the heart. Are we doing the same to others? Only the Lord sees us as complete in Him. If the world knew what we will look like when our Bridegroom comes for us, they would all want to come! As a priceless pearl is forged and beautified through years of friction and discomfort in a dark and isolated place, priceless lives are similarly forged and beautified in God's own refiner's fires of afflictions and testing! But again, God's word said, "O afflicted one, storm-tossed, and not comforted, behold, I will set your stones in antimony, and your foundations I will lay in sapphires. Moreover, I will make your battlements of rubies, and your gates of crystal, and your entire wall of precious stones" (Isa. 54:11–12)! Many of you today have been indoctrinated to believe, as I too once was, that your life is of no value or that you are too insignificant. Well, it's easy to believe that false narrative, but the truth is that you were made for so much more than you could possibly imagine, and those of whom the world and the devil have branded as damaged or worthless goods are often at the top of God's Most Wanted list.

Paul said this regarding letting go:

> Not that I have already obtained it or have already become perfect, but I press on so that I may lay hold of that for which also I was laid hold of by Christ Jesus. Brethren, I do not regard myself as having laid hold of it yet; but one thing I do: forgetting what lies behind and reaching forward to what lies ahead, I press on toward the goal for the prize of the upward call of God in Christ Jesus. (Phil. 3:12–14)

In addition, he said,

> For you see your calling, brethren, that not many wise according to the flesh, not many mighty, not many noble, are called. But God has chosen the foolish things of the world to put to shame the wise, and God has chosen the weak

things of the world to put to shame the things which are mighty; and the base things of the world and the things which are despised God has chosen, and the things which are not, to bring to nothing the things that are, that no flesh should glory in His presence. (1 Cor. 1:26–29)

Through everything—broken relationships, addiction, numerous weekends spent in different jails across the Midwestern part of the United States—nothing was able to separate me from the love of God in Christ Jesus! And through it all, Jesus Christ has taught me how there is no human life beyond God's infinite desire and zealous passion to love and to know. There's also no situation, pain, sin, or failure beyond His desire to forgive, heal, and restore. If we are willing to turn from our sins in true biblical repentance (Acts 3:19), commit our ways to the Lord, and trust also in Him (Ps. 37:4) through the ebb and flow of various seasons of our lives, God will inevitably shape us into the men and women we were always meant to be.

Like the demoniac before me, my life was a meaningless and very lonely existence. I was consumed with pain and bitter sorrows from over two decades of hard drug and alcohol abuse that began as my way of coping with the bitter anger I had bottled up inside of me toward my biological father. Yet all through the painful years, God had me surrounded by amazing people who relentlessly prayed for me, and like a broken record they would echo these words: "Ellis, Jesus is the answer. He loves you. He can turn your life around. Ellis, nothing is impossible for Him!" But contrary to their hopes and prayers, no one could do anything for me! What people couldn't understand was that I had spent moment by moment, day after day, and year after year crying out to Jesus, begging Him for help. And the older I got, the angrier I became. I thought, *If God is so good and has the infinite power to change my life as everyone says He does, then why is my life so empty, painful, and meaningless? Where is this Jesus when I need Him?* What I didn't know then that breaks my heart today is knowing all that my precious Lord and Savior had suffered for me! He too was despised, abandoned, and rejected by man—a

Man of sorrows and acquainted with grief. He bore my griefs and carried my sorrows. The Bible says He made Himself of no reputation, and, taking the form of a bondservant, He humbled Himself to become obedient to the point of death, even the death of the cross, to ransom me from a lifetime of slavery to sin and rebellion, a debt I could never pay. Jesus momentarily felt the full emotional effects of abandonment when He was brutally beaten and crucified between two thieves, and He cried out with a loud voice, saying, "Eli, Eli, lama sabachthani?" (that is, "My God, My God, why have You forsaken Me?"). He was left to die alone by His closest friends and was murdered by the people He came to save. Yes, Jesus paid the full price for my freedom, and it was by His stripes that I am now healed and restored. However, the one thing that Jesus could not do for me was choose Him. Fortunately for me, I made the right choice that day, and over the course of the next few years, God restored the lost years of my life (Joel 2:25). And like Job, He has blessed the latter days of my life far more than my beginning (Job 42:12).

CHAPTER 4

A BRUISED REED HE WILL NOT BREAK

I've always loved the way music has had that undeniable universal power to connect with the human experience. And one of the most moving songs I've ever heard is "Carried to the Table" by the Texas-based Christian rock band Leeland. In the way those incredibly special songs always do, the message of "Carried to the Table" not only connects with and lifts my spirit, but it also perfectly encapsulates my spiritual, emotional, and socially ravaged younger self when confronted by what every human being will inevitably encounter: a moment of truth! After years of increasingly intensified rebellion, I found myself crushed beneath the weight of my own iniquity and shattered by the fall. That song perfectly captures Ellis Lucas before Christ, a wounded young man, badly broken and feeling desperately alone, consumed with inner turmoil from what amounted to a self-inflicted broken life that I feared was so completely ruined that all hope for healing and restoration had passed me by and was beyond reach. But I couldn't have been more wrong, as it was there in my weakest moment when I heard my Savior calling me. I was lifted by His grace, comforted in His arms of love. What's more, both my life and my understanding of life were forever changed as I encountered the Lord's unmatchable power to liberate a bounded soul exactly as foretold in the Bible! And although I honestly don't have all the answers or understand many of the circumstances surrounding my life at that time, I unequivocally understand now how my new life in Jesus, like the demoniac of Mark chapter five, Joseph, and many in our own lifetime, is now an instrument in God's hands that He uses to encourage and testify before others to seek Him while He can still be found.

Are there still bad days, disappointments, and seasons of pain? Yes! But I accept them and have embraced how we must through many tribulations enter the kingdom of God (Acts 14:22b). "And not only that," says Paul, "but we also glory in tribulations, knowing that tribulation produces perseverance; and perseverance, character; and character, hope. Now hope does not disappoint, because the love of God has been poured out in our hearts by the Holy Spirit who was given to us" (Rom. 5:3–5). I pray each day for the grace to represent God as His workmanship in a worthy and honorable manner, just as Christ has done for me. Because what God has created out of the broken pieces of my life before knowing Jesus Christ is a tremendous example for why no one, for any reason, should ever compromise their heart's conviction. We don't have to accept failure, give in to loneliness or isolation or low self-esteem, get weighted down with feelings of being unwanted or unloved or rejected, or ever settle for defeat. Charles Haddon Spurgeon said this about suffering and trials: "Trials teach us what we are; they dig up the soil, and let us see what we are made of." He also said, "I would go to the deeps a hundred times to cheer a downcast spirit. It is good for me to have been afflicted, that I might know how to speak a word in season to one that is weary."

When I first put my trust in Jesus, I was a weak and feeble human being, still paranoid and badly broken emotionally, confined to a mental prison in my own mind because I rebelled against the Word of God and, quite frankly, grew to despise the counsel of the Most High God before coming to know Jesus as my Lord and Savior (Ps. 107:10–11). And although God had delivered and healed me of all my former addictions and was doing a tremendous work in my life, the first two years of my Christian life were undoubtedly among the hardest and most painful I have ever had to endure. I have said on many occasions that it wasn't the fear of God that kept me from committing suicide; it was the fear of hell and spending eternity there that kept me alive.

The first few months were by far the worst, just learning how naïve I had always been regarding Christianity as being a fairy-tale lifestyle where we'd all live happily ever after if I were ever to become a Christian. As I mentioned in my book *The Potter and the Clay*, I had encountered one preacher barking like a dog at one church while others were preaching very compelling messages about prosperity and being a millionaire. In any case, to say I was confused would be an understatement—and yes, I most certainly was.

However, two men stood out from the rest. One was Dr. George Westlake Jr., the senior pastor of Sheffield Family Life Center, an amazing church located in the very heart of the hood in Kansas City, Missouri. The church is completely multiracial in every area of the church, and people attend from over fifty miles every direction on Sundays. Sheffield Family Life Center also specializes in ministering to Kansas City's inner-city minorities and those with severely broken lives. One of my favorite things to do during those early days of walking with Jesus was to watch George and his precious wife, Jean, on their weekly television broadcast where they would take calls and answer people's questions about life and the Bible. I learned so much from listening to George and Jean breaking down life's challenging quandaries and dividing up the Word of God with such grace and boldness. I had never seen anything quite like them. I had seen Christian programs on television before but nothing like George and Jean's program.

Then a dear friend of mine asked me if I wanted to ride with him to Kansas City to visit Sheffield Family Life Center one Sunday morning, and of course I couldn't wait for the opportunity to hear Dr. Westlake preach a live sermon. But what I didn't expect was to have Dr. Westlake walk over to where we were seated, sit down at the seat next to me, and personally introduce himself to me when the church was filled with thousands of other people. Nor did I expect him to ask how my life was and if there was anything he or the church could do to minister to me! George continued to sit there and pour the love of Jesus into my severely wounded heart as though he could see right through me, even as the service started and his staff was signaling to him that it was time for him to begin his normal

Sunday morning preparation for sharing the message once the music had ended. Eventually, one of his staff members came over, interjected himself into the conversation, and then escorted Dr. Westlake backstage. George Westlake was more concerned about my welfare than he was about the enormous service going on around him, and that one act of genuine kindness was forever burned into the center of my heart and remains there to this day. I thank God for that precious moment in time that helped define the kind of Christian I wanted to be!

Then, some years later in 2010, when we were preparing for a weekend evangelistic outreach at the Black Hills State University in Spearfish, South Dakota, I asked Dr. Westlake if he would come to South Dakota and speak at the event. He didn't hesitate, and, in fact, he said that he would be honored to participate. When I picked him up at the airport, he smiled and asked me to quit calling him Dr. Westlake and to just call him George. Well, that's easier said than done when you have that much respect for someone, but nevertheless, I did my best because it was important to George that I understand that he is not Dr. Westlake to me now, but rather he is my friend—George Westlake Jr.

In John chapter fifteen, we find Jesus doing the same thing, saying,

> This is My commandment, that you love one another, just as I have loved you. Greater love has no one than this, that one lay down his life for his friends. You are My friends if you do what I command you. No longer do I call you slaves, for the slave does not know what his master is doing; but I have called you friends, for all things that I have heard from My Father I have made known to you. (John 15:12–15)

George is a portrait of the living Christ, who went to the land of the Gerasenes to extend His mercy and grace and healed and restored what's quite possibly the most extreme case of an outcast mentioned in the Bible apart from the Lord Himself: the demoniac. This was a tremendous public demonstration of Christ's humble heart and immeasurable love. That is what George Westlake did when he extended the healing power of Christ's redeeming love to what's quite possibly one of the most extreme cases of an outcast of modern times: Ellis Lucas!

The other pastor that stood out to me was Pastor Steve Poe, the senior pastor at Caring First Assembly in St. Joseph, Missouri, at that time. It seemed like every time I turned on my television I saw Pastor Steve talking about the church he pastored, Caring First Assembly, which was close to where I lived in St. Joseph, Missouri. Pastor Steve was constantly reaching out to the wounded, broken, hurting, and downcast—Christian or non—as he loved to share the love of God that is in Christ Jesus with all people, undoubtedly having a deep-seated compassion for the hurting. Furthermore, Steve is so passionate about loving the homeless, shut-ins, and forgotten members of our society that he, now located at Northview Church in Carmel, Indiana (the church he left Missouri to pastor a few months after my coming to faith in Jesus Christ), initiated a radical idea on how to not only bless their congregation but to do so with the intent of enabling them to bless others in need! Instead of receiving money, the ushers took the collection plate money, totaling over eighty-three thousand dollars, divided it up randomly into envelopes, and passed them out to the whole congregation. When interviewed, Pastor Steve told RTV6, "I don't care what you do with it. I don't care if you give it back to us or to a homeless person. I don't care what you do with it as long as you feel like you heard from God on what to do with it."

Steve is just as passionate about making disciples of both men and women, and like George Westlake Jr., there were simply no inconsistencies in Steve's walk. Not only was he a tremendous teacher, but also every time I entered the building for a church service, he would always take a minute to walk over, shake my hand, and say hello as he did to so many others as well. But the day he addressed the congregation at Caring First Assembly, saying that he and his wife would be leaving Caring First Assembly to move to Carmel, Indiana, I went to pieces as I began crying uncontrollably, devastated by the news. I had only been a Christian for a short while and couldn't imagine how I would survive without Pastor Steve's teaching and presence to help guide me to wherever it was that God was leading me.

Like Charles H. Spurgeon, Steve would also (and no doubt had already) go to the deeps at least a hundred times to cheer a downcast spirit. He told me that God was doing a great work in my life, that God had great plans for my life. I had heard that so many times before from my late mother, Mary Jeanette Lucas. This was different though, because it was substantiated by this remarkable man of God. Plus, I actually believed that God was working this all out for my good. Those few words not only fell on good soil, but they also sustained me for many years through thick and thin while God was transforming me—Ellis Lucas, the Christian—into the person I was created to be.

Both Steve and George were men of proven character, above reproach, and, like my late mother, both their word and reputation were impeccable. And although that brief season of observing Steve and George was short compared to the years I have enjoyed learning from my great friend Justin Alfred and others, they were very meaningful months. In addition, that season was instrumental in shaping my heart for the broken as well and helped prepare the way for the founding of His Heart United Network, a small nonprofit organization with a big vision to bring the healing heart of our wonderful God to a world of wounded individuals who desperately need to know they are loved, valued, needed, and wanted! And please understand—I don't believe either of these great men would ever approve of me writing a story like this if it was intended to glorify them, and neither would I. And that was never my intent. Rather, it is to say that God will never abandon us. In fact, for every Timothy or Titus there will always be the influence of a Paul, Lois, or Eunice in their lives. It was the example set before me by these two men that taught me; it's the kindness of the Lord that leads us to repentance (Rom. 2:4).

Most importantly, if we continue to show deep love for each other, love covers a multitude of sins (1 Pet. 4:8). I love to read quotes from Charles H. Spurgeon, the master of expressing deep spiritual thoughts through words. He too had a serious burden for the broken. Therefore, it shouldn't come as any surprise that he had his own struggles that taught him how to not just love others deeply but also how to express his thoughts so well in his writings. He battled depression so intense that, at times, he would have to leave his ministry for sometimes months to recover. He was a wounded healer and another great example of a man who put "Caring First" for the lost, broken, and hurting souls of this world above comfort, joy, and probably his own happiness. In fact, this moving quote says it all: "If sinners be damned, at least let them leap to Hell over our dead bodies. And if they perish, let them perish with our arms wrapped about their knees, imploring them to stay. If Hell must be filled, let it be filled in the teeth of our exertions, and let not one go unwarned and unprayed for."

Charles Spurgeon never saw himself as a great spiritual leader—which again, the great ones never do. I remember Pastor Steve sharing an unforgettable testimony about how he too had reluctantly agreed to temporarily fill in as the pastor at what became Caring First Assemblies. Steve shared how he never felt qualified, gifted, or comfortable with the idea of him being a pastor. He was a struggling local business owner who had no thought of being a pastor, and had the circumstances been any different, there may have never been a Pastor Steve Poe. In any case, Steve's sincere, transparent, and honest humility, combined with a genuine Christlike heart of compassion, left an enormous impression on thousands of broken hearts—and especially on mine. Steve taught me what it takes to change the world for another broken person! He taught me the difference between being a devout religious man and an extension of the mighty hand of Jesus Christ!

Matthew chapter twelve says,

> Look at my Servant, whom I have chosen.
> He is My Beloved, who pleases Me. I will put My
> Spirit upon Him, and He will proclaim justice
> to the nations. He will not fight or shout or raise
> His voice in public. A bruised reed He will not

break, and a smoldering wick He will not snuff out, till He has brought justice through to victory. In His name the nations will put their hope. (Matt. 12:18–21)

James said, "Religion that is pure and undefiled before God the Father is this: to visit orphans and widows in their affliction, and to keep oneself unstained from the world" (James 1:26).

I wonder how much of an impression Jesus's charitable life example left on James's heart, much in the same way that George Westlake Jr., Steve Poe, and Justin Alfred has made on mine? In addition, His Heart United is not, nor has it ever been, a group of miracle healers; we simply understand how sin, or needless suffering and loneliness, take no prisoners and show no mercy toward anyone. We also understand how a gracious word is like a honeycomb—sweetness to the soul and health to the body (Prov. 16:24)!

However, I can't say enough about how important it is to be in a healthy Bible-believing, Bible-teaching church where God can restore to you a confidence in His thoughts and love toward you, and where healing is not a momentary passing emotion that begins to fade before you get from the church building to your car to go home, but rather flows from a church where the pastor's personal doctrine regarding himself and his disciples says, "My life is worth nothing to me unless I use it for finishing the work assigned me by the Lord Jesus—the work of telling others the Good News about the wonderful grace of God. And now I know that none of you to whom I have preached the Kingdom will ever see me again. I declare today that I have been faithful. If anyone suffers eternal death, it's not my fault, for I didn't shrink from declaring all that God wants you to know. So guard yourselves and God's people. Feed and shepherd God's flock—His church, purchased with His own blood—over which the Holy Spirit has appointed you as leaders. I know that false teachers, like vicious wolves, will come in among you after I leave, not sparing the flock. Even some men from your own group will rise up and distort the truth in order to draw a following. Watch out! Remember the three years I was with you—my constant watch and care over you night and day, and my many tears for you. And now I entrust you to God and the message of His grace that is able to build you up and give you an inheritance with all those He has set apart for Himself" (Acts 20:24–32)!

God ordains certain trials and suffering to shape us into the people we were created to be. It is where we learn to both depend on and experience His faithfulness! But blessed be the God and Father of our Lord Jesus Christ, the Father of mercies and God of all comfort, who comforts us in all our affliction so that we will be able to comfort those who are in any affliction with the comfort with which we ourselves are comforted by God (2 Cor. 1:3–4). And as far as His Heart United in concerned, we not only care for the lost, broken, and hurting people of our generation, but most of us have also been through and experienced those deep valleys that many of you may be experiencing right now. We all sympathize with your weaknesses, just as Jesus Christ also sympathizes with our weaknesses still today. And yes, we are committed to bringing the healing of our amazing God to as many broken lives as the Lord will allow. Also, I pray that God will challenge you as you read this book and, moreover, that reading this book will challenge you to read your Bible and say, "Lord Jesus, make me to be what You will" and "Strengthen the hands that are weak and the knees that are feeble, and make straight paths for our feet, so that the limb which is lame may not be put out of joint, but rather be healed in You" (Heb. 12:12–13). Amen!

CHAPTER 5

LOVE THY ENEMIES

In my book *The Potter and the Clay*, I went to great lengths to make sure I didn't leave the impression, based on what God has done in my life, that God was some kind of genie in a bottle and that our every wish was His command. In fact, God is to be feared and honored and His plan for humanity taken seriously. Yes, what God has created from the broken pieces of my life before I knew Jesus Christ is amazing and simply unexplainable apart from God. But there is a story behind the story regarding my salvation, healing, and overall coveted relationship with Jesus Christ that is responsible for the amazing changes that accrued in my life—a beautiful relationship that I have loved and cherished more than anything in life. However, the story behind the story is always so difficult to explain because it involves complicated life decisions followed by commitment, healthy lifestyle arrangements, and discipline that will most certainly be tested.

I have listened to heart-wrenching accounts of parents whose kids got swept away by the swift and seductive currents of popular culture and, while trying to fit in or find acceptance, became imprisoned to alcoholism, addicted to heroin, methamphetamine, opioids, cocaine, or whatever the designer drug of the day may happen to be. Some are former honor roll students who dropped out of school as a result of their addictions. Some ran away from home and never returned. Others have gotten involved with gangs, while others got pregnant and either had an abortion or are living in a volatile situation trying to raise a baby in an unhealthy environment. These parents are understandably desperate for answers, never once expecting to see their child fall victim to Satan's strongholds. Furthermore, most of them did such a remarkable job at raising their children that they never anticipated any of these things affecting their families.

However, no one should ever assume they are beyond Satan's reach. Many of these precious young people were brought up in church as I was but slowly drifted away from God. They all have a tragic story that is both complicated and heartbreaking, and they all hope for the same miracle that lifted me from the gutter of human despair and restored my former shattered life! I have seen great victories for some, while others continue to sink deeper and deeper beneath the murky waters of hopelessness. The reason this is so important is because fulfillment and purpose according to God's plans for our lives (versus fulfillment and purpose according to our plans for our lives) may look very different at first. But notice I said *at first*, meaning temporary for those who set their minds on trusting God.

The dramatic story of Job in the Old Testament represents every broken life I am writing to and is a very accurate description of my own life after Jesus came into my life. Before I knew Jesus, Job's life and mine were nothing alike apart from possibly having some bigger-than-life influence in our early lives. Although it doesn't say, my thought is that Job must have had some kind of God-fearing parents or influence, which is why it is imperative for parents to understand why the Bible says to "Train up a child in the way he should go; even when he is old he will not depart from it" (Prov. 22:6), which means to train children in the fear and admonition of the Lord.

Jesus said, "I am the Way, the Truth, and the Life" (John 14:6)! But nonetheless, "The Lord said to Satan, 'Have you considered my servant Job, that there is none like him on the earth, a blameless and upright man, who fears God and turns away from evil?'" (Job 1:8). Job's life proves that godliness is no defense against adversity. Because although Job lived his life in a way that was pleasing to God, the Lord eagerly allowed Satan to test him. The most important aspect in Job's life was his faith in God. Remember, "Faith is the substance of things hoped for, the evidence of things not seen" (Heb. 11:6). Job had such an unbreakable faith, but by the same token, he also deeply feared and revered God (Job 1:1). That kind of reverence doesn't just happen—someone had imparted that fear in his heart!

Nonetheless, this testing cost Job his health, his wealth, and his family! And yes, this man was very wealthy in every way! "There were born to him seven sons and three daughters. He possessed seven thousand sheep, three thousand camels, five hundred yoke of oxen, and five hundred female donkeys, and very many servants, so that this man was the greatest of all the people of the east" (Job 1:2-3)! Imagine the morning and after-school chores going on if you were Job's kid! The Bible tells us that he was blameless, upright, fearing God, turning away from evil, and confronting and turning evil away. Job was also concerned with the spiritual condition of the next generation—of his own and of others (Job 1:4–5). His godly character manifested itself in his concern for the spiritual welfare of his children in that he offered burnt sacrifices to the Lord, interceding on behalf of those he loved to atone for their sins. But Job was also concerned for the welfare of the poor, the innocent, the orphan, and widow, saying, "I delivered the poor who cried for help," said Job, "and the orphan who had no helper. The blessing of the one ready to perish came upon me, and I made the widow's heart sing for joy. I put on righteousness, and it clothed me; my justice was like a robe and a turban. I was eyes to the blind and feet to the lame. I was a father to the needy, and I investigated the case which I did not know. I broke the jaws of the wicked and snatched the prey from his teeth" (Job 29:11–17).

So the question remains: why did God allow Satan to test such a righteous man? Well, in God's sovereign wisdom, He knows things we don't know. He can see events unfold in the future that we could have never even imagined. And we see that here when God asked Job,

> Where were you when I laid the foundations of the earth? Tell Me, if you have understanding. Who determined its measurements? Surely you know! Or who stretched the line upon

it? To what were its foundations fastened? Or
who laid its cornerstone, when the morning stars
sang together, and all the sons of God shouted
for joy? Or who shut in the sea with doors, when
it burst forth and issued from the womb; when I
made the clouds its garment, and thick darkness
its swaddling band; when I fixed My limit for it,
and set bars and doors; when I said, "This far you
may come, but no farther, and here your proud
waves must stop." (Job 38:4–11)

I encourage you to read the entire book of Job, but especially
read chapter thirty-eight, where this staggering list goes on and on!
It will certainly help put things back in perspective for you. But God
knew Job would remain faithful and that his story would inspire millions of faithful Christians to persevere in their trials throughout the
ages, and my hope is that it will do the same for you in your trials!

However, it is crucial to note the sequence of events up to this
point, because the greatest test undoubtedly had to be the betrayal of
Job's friends (Job 4–31) and perhaps being rebuked by his own wife.
"Then his wife said to him, 'Do you still hold fast your integrity?
Curse God and die.' But he said to her, 'You speak as one of the foolish women would speak. Shall we receive good from God, and shall
we not receive evil?'" (Job 2:9–10). Again, what did Jesus say?

Do not love the world or the things in the
world. If anyone loves the world, the love of the
Father is not in him. For all that is in the world—
the desires of the flesh and the desires of the eyes
and pride of life—is not from the Father but is
from the world. And the world is passing away
along with its desires, but whoever does the will
of God abides forever. (1 John 2:15–17)

Instead of supporting her husband in his downfall, Job's wife
proceeds to judge him and debilitate him in his weakness. And it

is only when Job obeys God and intercedes on behalf of his three friends who had now become his enemies that God blesses Job with a twofold inheritance (42:8–17). The story ends with Job's health and fortune being restored along with another ten children! Job's "reward" was not at all some kind of consolation prize for his unfair treatment; rather, it was the inheritance God promises to all who serve faithfully as redemptive agents of the Creator (Dan. 12:3).

Job obeyed God and was rewarded for his obedience! I completely agree that healing does require a genuine faith, although this shouldn't be "faith in faith" for the sake of placing your hope in a temporary sign, miracle, or wonder that can be so deceptive. For false Christs and false prophets will appear and perform great signs and miracles to deceive even the elect—if that were possible (Matt. 24:24). And the coming of the lawless one is according to the working of Satan, with all power, signs, and lying wonders (2 Thess. 2:9). Instead, the kind of faith that I am suggesting is a faith that confidently accepts the plans God has for your life, sight unseen, causing you to know that the Father's plans for you are for good and that not of evil, to give you a future with hope (Jer. 29:11).

Again, we know that hope that is seen is not hope; for who hopes for what they already see (Rom. 8:24)! We also know that faith is the substance of things hoped for, the evidence of things not yet seen (Heb. 11:1)! The riches of the glory of this mystery among all who believe on Him is Christ in us, the hope of glory (Col. 1:27).

Yet, in any case, when I start talking about victory through submission or power made perfect in weakness or the unthinkable, like "loving your enemies," the mood suddenly begins to fade and hearts begin to sink! Undoubtedly, this wisdom would sound absurd to some people, but God says, "My thoughts are not your thoughts, nor are your ways My ways," declares the Lord. "For as the heavens are higher than the earth, so are My ways higher than your ways and My thoughts than your thoughts" (Isa. 55:8–9). Additionally, Paul wrote, "If anyone among you seems to be wise in this age, let him become a fool that he may become wise. For the wisdom of this world is foolishness with God" (1 Cor. 3:18–20). That is why Paul emphatically said to not be conformed to this world any longer but to be transformed by the renewing of your mind. This is done through the process of sanctification, where God cleanses our thoughts and minds by the washing of water by the Word of God (Eph. 5:26), and according to His mercy by the washing of regeneration and renewing by the Holy Spirit (Titus 3:5). And even though He was Jesus Christ, God incarnate, and the only begotten Son of God, He learned obedience from the things which He suffered (Heb. 5:6–7).

The greatest test for me since becoming a Christian has been learning to love my enemies. And let's be real about this—they are called enemies for a reason because they don't like us, and their intentions and actions demonstrate their feelings toward us. Loving my enemies goes against every ounce of understanding or willingness I ever had! In the Bible, though, there are numerous stories of God's people under fire along with the detailed accounts of those individuals who conquered numerous impossible situations that have made their testimonies legendary. These were people just like you and me—sinners saved by grace, saints by the eternal will of God, but legends by denying themselves and allowing the strength of Almighty God to be their fortress and defense!

At other times, while crushed beneath a weight of emotions and fear, many individuals have been driven far from the core of God's power and grace, unable to obey the wisdom and trust the counsel that would have purified their faith and changed them from the inside out—the very pit of hopelessness and despair. God has committed to all believers the Word of reconciliation, which is the Gospel. Therefore, we are ambassadors for Christ, set apart and empowered by God to preach this awesome news as though God were making an appeal through us on behalf of Christ to be reconciled to God (2 Cor. 5:17–20). But if we love only those who love us in return then we're no better off than (and no more useful to the kingdom of God than) a talking donkey. Furthermore, if the rocks have to cry out because the church went silent, then this world and our country is in big trouble and guilty of trampling underfoot the blood of Jesus Christ that was shed for the whole world, including our enemies!

But if God's people who are called by His name will humble themselves and pray and sincerely seek His face and turn from their wicked ways, God said, "Then, I will hear from heaven and will forgive their sin and heal their land" (2 Chron. 7:14). The best way to get rid of an enemy is to make them your friend in Jesus! Remember what Jesus told His disciples? "With man this is impossible, but with God all things are possible" (Matt. 19:26). Humility is the opposite of pride, the very poison that got Satan cast out of heaven, caused the fall, and sent Jesus Christ to the cross. Prayer is a dialogue with God; however, 2 Chronicles 7:14 is asking for more than just a normal dialogue with God—it requires seeking God with all your heart!

God said for people to humble themselves, "Pray, and seek My face!" This is acknowledging how we alone are responsible for the questionable decisions we have made that have hurt or damaged our lives, and that we acknowledged that we can't do this on our own—that we need God and that only God Himself is able. Furthermore, we alone have the authority to make the decision to humble ourselves beneath the mighty hand of God in recognition of His sovereign authority over all things and to profess our faith in Him as the supreme and final authority over all things. That will result in the restoration of the lost years of our lives!

For instance, let's say that someone was abandoned by their spouse and badly hurt by the betrayal. So, the question is: were they following Christ when they made the decision to marry that person, and, if so, were they equally yoked? Perhaps they were both following Christ and in the eyes of God and man were equally yoked, and despite doing everything right, their marriage still came unraveled. Was the committed person able to forgive as Christ forgave them, or did that individual become bitter and plunge headlong into an ocean of sin? You see why this is so difficult to explain? But this is the story regarding what happened that restored hope, brought healing, and completely transformed my life. After we acknowledge and then take responsibility for our own actions and confession is made, the act must be followed up with repentance: "Turn from their wicked ways!" God says that when that happens, He will hear from heaven and will forgive their sin and heal their land—or, in this case, as many single individuals as will keep His word, commit their way to Him, and trust Him! "You then, my child, be strengthened by the grace that is in Christ Jesus, and what you have heard from me in the presence of many witnesses entrust to faithful men, who will be able to teach others also" (Tim. 2:1–2).

Are we worthy of such honor? No! We are sinful creatures, and our consciences have a funny way of reminding us of what kind of people we are. But God sees the finished work He has begun in each of us, and even though we are sinners, the Lord says, "Come now, and let us reason together. Though your sins are like scarlet, they shall be as white as snow; though they are red like crimson, they shall be as wool" (Isa. 1:18).

My friend Ed Lococo will often become overwhelmed by the goodness of God and in an emotional moment will say, "Ellis, I feel so unworthy of God's goodness!" My response is always, "If we felt any other way, I would be seriously concerned." I always remind him of the two men who went up to the temple to pray—the one being a Pharisee and the other a tax collector.

> The Pharisee stood and prayed thus with himself, "God, I thank You that I am not like other men—extortioners, unjust, adulterers, or even as this tax collector. I fast twice a week; I give tithes of all that I possess." And the tax collector, standing afar off, would not so much as raise his eyes to heaven, but beat his breast, saying, "God, be merciful to me a sinner!" The Lord said: "I tell you, this man [the tax collector] went down to his house justified rather than the other; for everyone who exalts himself will be humbled, and he who humbles himself will be exalted." (Luke 18:10–14)

Remember: "If we have died with Him, we will also live with Him; if we endure, we will also reign with Him; if we deny Him, He also will deny us; if we are faithless, He remains faithful" (2 Tim.

2:11–13)! And finally, "To Him who is able to do far more abundantly beyond all that we ask or think, according to the power that works within us, to Him be the glory in the church and in Christ Jesus to all generations forever and ever. Amen" (Eph. 3:20)!

CHAPTER 6

WHOM SHALL I SEND, WHO WILL GO FOR US?

People have often asked, "Ellis, how can you and Peggi continue to love the ministry so much when, at times, it is exhausting, painful, and costly?" And I fully understand what they're asking because ministry isn't always a sunny walk in the park. But then again, what in life isn't exhausting, painful, or costly? Furthermore, I don't really see what Peggi and I do as a ministry, even though I am president of His Heart United Ministries, an organization we founded. Instead, this is our life and yes, we love it!

I love to share the story about an event we did that took place at the Black Hills State University in Spearfish, South Dakota. One of my dearest friends, Justin Alfred, was speaking, and one of the most amazing young Christian rock bands on the planet, Bread of Stone, was preforming at the event. Bill and Ben, along with their father, Nehemiah, formed the band—or, in this case, ministry—which has since become a powerful international outreach where God has, through their service, reached thousands of lost and broken souls all around the world. And what most people may not know is that this amazing family is comprised of former Muslims. Their mother is a native of Iran, and their father, Nehemiah, is from Indonesia. Their family story is simply amazing, especially their salvation story.

While their father, Nehemiah, had been reading his Koran, God began speaking into his heart the truth about His Son, Jesus Christ, and the cross upon which He died for his sins. Nehemiah invited Jesus Christ to come into his heart and be Lord and Savior of his life and also to reach his family. The rest is history. But during his presentation, Justin Alfred began to explain how Bill, Ben, and their family could no longer return to their mother's home country to visit family or friends, or else they would run the risk of being arrested and quite possibly executed for converting to Christianity. That silenced the auditorium and hit me like a ton of bricks. Here in America we take the Bible and family for granted. But in certain places around the world, Bibles are illegal to own and converting to Christianity is considered a capital crime. What's more, converting to Christianity can result in an even more severe form of abandonment—the disownment and alienation from your family.

That was the case of Sherzod Odilov, a foreign exchange student from Uzbekistan. Sherzod did not anticipate the high price he would pay for the decision he made to follow Jesus Christ, but knowing the price that Jesus Christ paid for him, Sherzod stands firm on his decision. When Sherzod, who graduated from Jacksonville (Ark.) High School, telephoned his Muslim parents in Uzbekistan to tell them of his newfound faith in Jesus Christ, his own father disowned him, making it clear that he was no longer welcome in his home and was never again to speak to his mother or his siblings. He withdrew all funds from Sherzod's U.S. bank account, arranged to cancel his son's U.S. sponsorship and college scholarship, and even drew up legal papers declaring Sherzod is no longer his son.

As devastating as that must be for anyone—especially an eighteen-year-old young man located halfway around the world from his biological family—Sherzod remains strong in his commitment to Christ. "I am not sorry I accepted Jesus Christ," he said. "I am not sorry for getting baptized. Even though my parents did that, I am not sorry for anything that happened." I remember talking to brothers Ben and Bill after the South Dakota event and confessed how I had never taken into consideration the high cost Muslims pay for becoming Christians and how it broke my heart to know how much they had given in exchange for their obedience in following Jesus Christ!

Their response was equally stunning as they smiled and said, "Ellis, we didn't lose anything when we accepted Jesus Christ.

Everything was already lost without Him. What you are missing is that, because of what Jesus Christ gave in return for our salvation—His life in exchange for ours on the cross—we gained everything!" Wow, that sure brings things into perspective. It is imperative that we keep things in perspective regarding life, ministry, and especially our personal relationship with our Lord and Savior, Jesus Christ. Because when you understand how this present dark age in which we currently live is only the conception of what we are to become, not only will you not lose heart when facing various hardships, but you will also learn to count it all joy, knowing that in due season you will reap what you have sown if you keep your eyes fixed on Jesus and never give up.

We are instructed to be steadfast, immovable, always abounding in the work of the Lord, knowing that our toil is not in vain in the Lord (1 Cor. 15:58). This present dark and congested life is like being alive but oblivious to what's beyond the here and now. In many respects, it is similar to being confined to the limits of our mother's womb. In a comparable way, we are all being carried through this short term we call life, kicking and struggling, trying to break loose and break free, somehow sensing that we are not created to remain in this dark, limited space forever. Our hearts tell us that we are created for so much more than this. Then, on that glorious day when our term is complete, the womb of this life will open up, and we will pass from this life into the next where, for the believers, heaven will erupt with shouts of joy, celebrating, and ecstatic excitement for the opportunity to welcome us into heaven and eternity without the struggles and limits of this present life. Family will be there holding us, taking family photos and passing us around after Jesus has had His opportunity to first hold us in His gentle arms and wipe away every tear from our eyes and welcome us into our Father's magnificent home where there will be no more death—neither sorrow, nor crying, nor any more pain. In other words, we have not yet even begun to live life. "Eye hath not seen, nor ear heard, neither have entered into the heart of man, the things which God hath prepared for them that love Him" (1 Cor. 2:9)!

So, for now, let us also fix our eyes on Jesus through the eyes of faith, the author, perfecter, and finisher of faith, who for the joy set before Him endured the cross, despising the shame, and has sat down at the right hand of the throne of God. For consider Him who has endured such violence and hostility by sinners against Himself. One thing worse than enduring the pain of giving life through natural childbirth is to be crucified on a wooden cross to give us new life in heaven with Him forever. Remember also that those who sow in tears now shall reap with joyful shouting. Those who go to and fro weeping, carrying their bag of seed, shall indeed come again with a shout of joy, bringing his sheaves with him (Ps. 126:5–6). "We know that our light afflictions, which are but for a moment, are working for us a far more exceeding and eternal weight of glory" (2 Cor. 4:16–17).

What I love even more about Ben, Bill, and their family is how we all share a common thread, a heart desire for the lost and broken people of our generation, that they too might know, love, and make known who is the universal healer and Great Physician, Jehovah Rapha, God our healer. The late American evangelist Jim Elliot, who lost his life when he traveled to Ecuador in 1956 to introduce the Auca Indian tribe to the Bible and the Christian faith, made this timeless and remarkable statement: "He is no fool who gives what he cannot keep, to gain that which he cannot lose."

I've always known that what God has done in my life was no accident. It was a very intentional demonstration of His grace, power, and love! My life represents an undeniable example of His heart toward all people, but especially those wounded and forsaken. It serves as a reminder that hope, healing, and total restoration is never further than a single prayer away at any given time. It proves that nothing is impossible with God (Luke 1:37)! I titled this chapter "Whom Shall I Send" because of the many parallels between the illustration in the sixth chapter of Isaiah and my own personal encounter with the Lord on March 6, 1997. I also chose this title because of a message in the text concerning you. Isaiah's encounter illustrates what can only be seen through the eyes of faith, the literal purging of sin, the rebirth of the human soul. Unlike Isaiah, however,

I never saw the throne room or face of God, but the experience was very similar in many ways.

One thing that caught my attention was the coal that touched Isaiah's lips in verses 6–7, resulting in the instant purging of Isaiah's iniquities (Isa. 6:6–7). That immediately took me back to my encounter with my Lord and Savior, and how I too was touched, healed, and forgiven. I too was instantly purged of twenty-four years of drug and alcohol addiction, anger, and violence, and was completely cleansed of a lifetime of rebellion! It also helps answer the most puzzling question that any of us would have on our minds in that situation: "Why me?"

In fact, my exact thought was, how could God love someone like me, and why would God choose me to represent Him when there are so many far better, more qualified candidates to choose from? Why did God choose to pour out His infinite mercy and blessing on me, a former drug addict and alcoholic with countless other deeply painful and regretful failures in my past? What did God see in the lives of so many people with questionable pasts, such as Paul, Moses, or David, an adulterer and murderer, yet branded by God as a man after His own heart? What about Matthew the tax collector or Mary Magdalene? Together, we have a combined laundry list of sins that includes everything from prostitution, murder, theft, adultery, sorcery, witchcraft, bitter hearts consumed with envy hatred, and so on. We were law breakers, whoremongers, and criminals. Moreover, by today's standards, we were all society's rejects.

In my book *The Potter and the Clay*, I documented in detail the remarkable journey that God brought me through in pursuit of my life, allowing me to experience the sting of rebellion, isolation, and emptiness along with loneliness and unimaginable pain that comes from being a self-absorbed humanistic pig whose sole desire was instant gratification and worldly pleasure. I was too far out of touch with reality to know that I was on a fast track to destruction and in danger of the fires of hell! I never gave any thought to the consequences I would one day bear. However, that all changed when Jesus Christ came to my rescue and disclosed the seriousness of my situation, the danger I was in, and the costly consequences I was facing—and then, shockingly, offered me an alternative.

God unveiled the mystery that my mother seemed to know about during my childhood—the calling I had never seriously contemplated or believed, despite her predictions, or even thought possible. But just as she predicted, God, in fact, did have a distinct purpose for my life (Eph. 2:10). Nonetheless, the question remained: why would God, Who created the universe and everything in it, Who has searched me and known me better than I know myself, still consciously choose me to be His ambassador to a fallen world when I was probably worse off than most of my contemporaries? What's more, if you were to ask me back then, I would have said that almost any other human being alive would have been a more logical choice as an ambassador than me.

Psalm 139 says that God knows my sitting down and my rising up, and He understands my every thought afar off, and the same is true for you. He comprehends our paths and our lying down, and is acquainted with all our ways. There's not a word on our tongues, but behold, He knows it altogether! So why then would Jesus Christ, Who knows my every pain, sin, thought, flaw, weakness, and failure, pursue a personal and meaningful love relationship with someone like me? I sincerely believe the answer is, in part, found in Isaiah 6:5 and 6:8, where Isaiah—an ordinary, everyday guy—suddenly and unexpectedly is caught up in the presence of the Lord, and in a moment of shock and fear, he shouts, "Woe is me, for I am undone, for I am a man of unclean lips, and I dwell in the midst of a people of unclean lips; for my eyes have seen the King, the Lord of hosts" (Isa. 6:5)!

Jewish people of that era had a common belief that was based on a personal encounter Moses had with God that was recorded in Exodus 33:20, that no flesh could stand in the presence of God and survive His holiness. God said to Moses, "You cannot see My face, for no man can see Me and live!" Imagine the shock Isaiah must have felt when God's response to him was, "Well, then, whom shall I send? Likewise, who will go for Us?" (Isa. 6:8). I believe this is a reference to the very catalyst for which our Christian faith is founded. "For as it is written," says the Apostle Paul, "there are none righteous, not even one" (Rom. 3:10). "All have sinned and fallen short of the glory of God" (Rom. 3:23).

I believe that what God is saying is, "If not you, Isaiah, then who?" No human being is worthy or qualified to handle those things consecrated unto God. However, God doesn't call the qualified; He qualifies the called and then sanctifies them to Himself through the Word of truth (John 17:17). But having the faith or spiritual eyes to see past the criteria others think should be met to qualify a person for spiritual leadership is another thing altogether. However, the Lord does not see as man sees, as was the case with David and Gideon being chosen; for man looks at the outward appearance, but the Lord looks at the heart (1 Sam. 16:7).

You might be surprised to learn that, although being chosen by God for the apostleship to replace the Lord's betrayer, Judas Iscariot, the Apostle Paul encountered his own share of difficulties in the area of acceptance from the other eleven apostles as well as other Christians. Yes, even Paul, the great apostle who wrote two-thirds of the New Testament, encountered opposition, rejection, and resistance. For example, Jesus appeared in a vision to a disciple in Damascus named Ananias and told him to go to Saul (the former name of Paul). Ananias was afraid because he knew of Saul's reputation as a merciless persecutor of the church.

Saul of Tarsus was a known Pharisee in Jerusalem who, after the crucifixion and resurrection of Jesus Christ, swore to wipe out the new Christian movement. He was present when they stoned Stephen to death for preaching a powerful and compelling historical and moving message until he decided to end his message by indicting the crowds with these stinging words of truth:

> You stiff-necked people, uncircumcised in heart and ears, you always resist the Holy Spirit. As your fathers did, so do you. Which of the prophets did your fathers not persecute? And they killed those who announced beforehand the coming of the Righteous One, Whom you have now betrayed and murdered, you who received

the law as delivered by angels and did not keep it.
(Acts 7:51–53)

But as they were stoning Stephen, he called out, "Lord Jesus, receive my spirit." And, falling to his knees, he cried out with a loud voice, "Lord, do not hold this sin against them." After he had said this, he died and was credited for being the first Christian martyr (Acts 7:59–61).

Shortly thereafter in Acts 9:1, Saul began breathing out murderous threats against the Lord's disciples. He obtained letters from the high priest, authorizing him to arrest any followers of Jesus in the city of Damascus. After his conversion, Saul changed his name to Paul. Naturally, people would have some doubt regarding the legitimacy of Paul's conversion—and even more doubt concerning his claim to the apostleship by way of a revelation from Jesus Christ Himself! The other remaining apostles believed that Matthias was God's choice to replace Judas, and therefore they rejected Paul.

For years, Paul was considered an outsider and was not fully accepted by the remaining apostles. However, he was far more prominent than Matthias—and was also more prominent than any of the remaining eleven apostles, except for perhaps Peter and maybe John. What's more, Paul would not have been qualified based on the apostle's own criteria.

"For it is written in the Book of Psalms: 'Let another take his office' (referring to Judas Iscariot). Therefore (the apostle's criteria), of these men who have accompanied us all the time that the Lord Jesus went in and out among us, beginning from the baptism of John to that day when He was taken up from us, one of these must become a witness with us of His resurrection." And they proposed two: Joseph called Barsabas, who was surnamed Justus, and Matthias. And they prayed and said, "You, O Lord, Who know the hearts of all, show which of these two You have chosen to take part in this ministry and apostleship from which Judas by transgression fell, that he might go to his own place." And they cast their lots, and the lot fell on Matthias. And he was numbered with the eleven apostles. (Acts 1:20–26)

Paul never accompanied them all the time that Jesus was with them. In fact, I don't believe he accompanied them any of the time Jesus was with them, nor did he witness the actual resurrection with them. That could be why Paul, in the opening verse of the book of Galatians, began this way: "Paul, an apostle (not sent from men nor through the agency of man, but through Jesus Christ and God the Father, Who raised Him from the dead)" (Gal. 1:1).

In Saul's moment of truth, he quickly understood that Jesus was indeed the true Messiah and that he (Saul) had helped murder and imprison innocent people. Saul realized that despite his previous beliefs as a Pharisee, he now knew the truth about God and was obligated to obey Him. Paul's conversion proves that God can call and transform anyone He chooses, even the most hard-hearted individual, to represent His kingdom. I especially love this story because of how it also demonstrates God's infinite mercy triumphing over our sin and the power of Hid redeeming love. God may have intentionally called Paul in this particular way for our benefit, to teach us the valuable lesson that it's better to trust in the Lord than to put confidence in man (Ps. 118:8)! For the Lord will be your confidence and will keep your foot from being caught (Prov. 3:26)! Yet, in any case, we are to test the spirits to see whether they are from God, because many false prophets have gone out into the world (1 John 4:1). "And no wonder! For Satan, himself transforms himself into an angel of light" (2 Cor. 11:14)!

Nonetheless, we are God's workmanship created in Christ Jesus for good works, which God hath foreordained that we should walk in them (Eph. 2:10). And whom He foreknew, He also predestined to be conformed to the image of His Son, that He might be the first-born among many brethren. And whom He predestined, these He also called; whom He called, these He also justified; and whom He justified, these He also glorified (Rom. 8:26–30)! All this means is that God already had a purpose in mind for your life just as He did for Paul, me, and every other human being ever created. We are justified, called, and chosen because of the finished work of Jesus Christ on the cross and how we respond to the Gospel. But the choice to accept God's plan for our lives or reject it is ours. However, the consequences for the choices we make are determined by God. Doubt, fear, and unbelief are not acceptable excuses for not trusting God. "For since the creation of the world His invisible *attributes* are clearly seen, being understood by the things that are made, *even* His eternal power and Godhead, so that they are without excuse" (Rom. 1:20, emphasis added).

When God said He would forgive, heal, and restore my broken life if I would commit my life to Him and trust Him, my question to Him was, "Why? Why would You do something like that for someone like me?" His simple response was this: "Because I love you!" I knew in my heart there was only one choice—the choice that changed my life forever. But that choice to accept God's pardon or reject it during that moment of truth was my responsibility. It was the difference between discovering and living the divine purpose for which I was created, or merely existing in a world and cosmos created by God for extraordinary life far beyond imagination and yet never really living this life at all!

Finally, not only are you dearly loved and wanted, but God promises that

> As the rain and the snow come down from heaven, and do not return to it without watering the earth and making it bud and flourish, so that it yields seed for the sower and bread for the eater, so is My Word that goes out from My mouth: it will not return to Me empty but will accomplish what I desire and achieve the purpose for which I sent it. (Isa. 55:10–11)
>
> He has swallowed up death for all time, and the Lord God will one day soon wipe tears away

from all of His true followers, He will remove the reproach of His people from all the earth; For the Lord has spoken. (Isa. 25:8)

CHAPTER 7

DELIGHT YOURSELF ALSO IN THE LORD

I have never met a single human being who purposely set out to destroy their lives or embrace the reality of a broken family or a ruined life. Undoubtedly, though, it does happen, and when it does, the results are usually catastrophic. By the same token, I have never met a contrite believer in Jesus who passed through the fires of God's refining afflictions that now regret the magnification of their faith and the augmentation of their strength to overcome adversity and conquer life's merciless and unforgiving trials and tribulations that will inevitably come upon us all, to both test us and humble us in order to reveal what's in our hearts!

Suffering is never pleasant for the moment; however, it can be an unforeseen gift from God in that, although hardships may take a toll on a person, their family, and possibly even their coveted life achievements, they can also have a purifying effect on our hearts and minds by exposing the futility of pursuing the wrong desires or putting trust in the temporary passing pleasures of this life—especially if it means losing or being presumptuous regarding the true riches of this life. We often take for granted God, our families, our freedom, and even our health until something goes awry. There are countless things we tend to put on the backburner of our lives that unexpected tragedies often reveal are most important. Hardships can awaken us to the reality that there is more to life than the here and now and can have a focus effect on our hearts and minds that remind us of our inability to achieve contentment or a purpose-filled life apart from our Creator and Designer.

God will undoubtedly take advantage of any and all situations that may humble us and cause us to turn to Him for answers. It's so easy to lose ourselves in the world's popular but temporal pursuits and slowly lose sight of life itself. Therefore, God will allow us to incur certain difficulties along the way that are meant to hopefully bring us back to the heart of what really matters—an undivided heart of worship and a life fully and unashamedly devoted to Him. Success kept in perspective can be a wonderful blessing, but no matter how much wealth one has accumulated, apart from God, money will never be able to buy you a single second of true and lasting happiness. However, it can, in fact, cost you everything!

There is a story in the Gospel of Luke that describes this very scenario and exposes the true nature of many human hearts regarding what I will refer to as blind idolatry. And sadly, it's just as true in the hearts of certain leaders within the religious community, as was the case with the story of the rich young ruler when encountering his own moment of truth. According to Luke, there was a religious leader who once asked Jesus this question: "Good Teacher, what should I do to inherit eternal life?" "Why do you call me good?" Jesus asked him. "Only God is truly good."

Apparently this individual must have had some idea about the true identity of Jesus and seemed to be a very devout religious man. Nevertheless, Jesus said,

> "To answer your question, you know the commandments: 'You must not commit adultery. You must not murder. You must not steal. You must not testify falsely. Honor your father and mother.'" The man replied, "I've obeyed all these commandments since I was young." When Jesus heard his answer, He said, "There is still one thing you haven't done. Sell all your possessions and give the money to the poor, and you will have treasure in heaven. Then come, follow Me."

But when the man heard this, he became very sad, for he was very rich. When Jesus saw this, He said, "How hard it is for the rich to enter the Kingdom of God! In fact, it is easier for a camel to go through the eye of a needle than for a rich person to enter the Kingdom of God!" Those who heard this said, "Then who in the world can be saved?" He replied, "What is impossible for people is possible with God." (Luke 18:18–27)

Wow! Was this not a near repeat of what later happened with the Apostle Paul? Both were devout religious leaders who had accomplished great measures of success, and, by the world's standards, this particular religious leader would have no doubt been the people's choice. He had money and great wealth, and appeared very pious by keeping every commandment since he was a child, except for the one that says, "I am the Lord your God, Who brought you out of the land of Egypt, out of the house of bondage. You shall have no other gods before Me" (Exod. 20:2). This promising young man unfortunately succumbed to the house of bondage through the love of money (blind idolatry). Furthermore, James said, "Whosoever shall keep the whole law, and yet offend in one point, he is guilty of all. For He that said, do not commit adultery, said also, do not kill. Now if thou commit no adultery, yet if thou kill, thou art become a transgressor of the whole law" (James 2:10–11).

Neither heaven nor God's manifold blessing is based on or acquired through works or merit. On the other hand, notice Paul's reaction after a face-to-face encounter with his own moment of truth and the difference between his heart and the rich young ruler's. Paul said,

I thank Christ Jesus our Lord, Who has given me strength [through the fires of afflictions] to do His work. He considered me trustworthy and appointed me to serve Him, even though I used to blaspheme the name of Christ.

In my ignorance, I persecuted His people. But God had mercy on me because I did it in ignorance and in unbelief. Oh, how generous and gracious our Lord was! He filled me with the faith and love that come from Christ Jesus. This is a trustworthy saying, and everyone should accept it: "Christ Jesus came into the world to save sinners"—and I am the worst of them all. But God had mercy on me so that Christ Jesus could use me as a prime example of His great patience with even the worst sinners. Then because of the great work God has done in my life, others will realize that they, too, can believe in Him and receive eternal life. All honor and glory to God forever and ever! (1 Tim. 1:12–17)

That could have just as easily been said about my testimony or that of the demoniac from Mark chapter five or that of so many wonderful people throughout world history. Jesus is the eternal King in glory, the unseen one Who never dies, Who alone is God. Amen. There is a significant difference between knowing God and zealously desiring to commit one's life to Him, pursue His will, and give all for His good pleasure, and being a devout religious person seeking the benefits of heaven by keeping the law and by doing good works but having little or no interest in our blessed Redeemer and Savior, Jesus Christ.

"In the same way," says Luke, the beloved physician who accompanied Paul continuously for two years but also records the Lord's counsel, saying, "Those of you who do not give up everything you have cannot be My disciples" (Luke 14:33). Now, the Lord isn't speaking in literal terms, no more than He was a few verses back where He made these puzzling comments: "If anyone comes to Me and does not hate father and mother, wife and children, brothers and sisters, yes, even their own life, such a person cannot be My disciple. And whoever does not carry their cross and follow Me cannot be My disciple" (Luke 14:20–27).

We know that our Lord is not commanding us to literally hate our parents or siblings. In Ephesians 6:1–2, He tells us to obey our parents in the Lord, for this is what is right. He said for us to honor our fathers and mothers, which is the fifth of the God's Ten Commandments but the first commandment promising that if we do so it may go well with us and that we may enjoy long life on the earth. Likewise, what Jesus is saying is this: "Where your treasure is, there your heart will be also" (Matt. 6:21). If material wealth is where our heart is, the Lord says we are not worthy to be His disciples (Luke 14:33).

The legendary singer/songwriter and rock music icon Bob Dylan wrote a huge hit song about that topic called "Gotta Serve Somebody." The main line of the song Dylan sings says, "It may be the devil or it may be the Lord, but you're gonna have to serve somebody!" Matthew, the writer of the Gospel that bears his name, knew the temptation of covetousness through his own struggles with a love for money and the riches of this world from his days working as a Roman tax collector. That may be why he wrote a similar line in his Gospel, saying, "No one can serve two masters. For you will hate one and love the other; you will be devoted to one and despise the other."

Matthew undoubtedly experienced the addictive struggles with money, which is most likely the reason he took a job collecting taxes for the despised Roman government. It was a well-known fact that a tax collector could make a fortune by overtaxing—in other words, choosing whatever amount they wanted to charge. During the time of Jesus in first-century Israel, there were publicans and tax collectors who could walk up to a man and tax him for what he was carrying— and so much more. Imagine that! These tax collectors were hated and despised because they were more often than not fellow Jews, as was the case with Matthew. These individuals were considered traitors that sold their souls to work for the Roman government.

No one would have understood this principle more than Matthew, who went on to say, "You cannot serve God and be enslaved to money" (Matt. 6:24). Matthew knew that the love of money is a root of all kinds of evil, for which some, including himself, have strayed from the faith in greediness and pierced themselves through with many sorrows (1 Tim. 6:10). Matthew learned that to know Jesus is to know contentment, the one thing that cannot be measured in dollars and cents (1 Tim. 6:6).

In Mark chapter eight, Jesus began to teach His disciples that He, the Son of Man, must suffer many things, that He would be rejected by the elders and chief priests and scribes, and would be brutally killed, and after three days rise again. That brings things into perspective. Jesus knew the unthinkable cost He would have to pay for our redemption; it would cost Him His own broken body and shed blood on that cross at Calvary. He responded in kind when He called the people to Himself, with His disciples also, and said to them,

> Whoever desires to come after Me, let him deny himself, and take up his cross, and follow Me. For whoever desires to save his life will lose it, but whoever loses his life for My sake and the gospel's will save it. For what will it profit a man if he gains the whole world, and loses his own soul? Or what will a man give in exchange for his soul? For whoever is ashamed of Me and My words in this adulterous and sinful generation, of him the Son of Man also will be ashamed when He comes in the glory of His Father with the holy angels. (Mark 8:34–38)

By permission I borrowed the following paragraph from one of my favorite and trusted Bible answer resource websites, GotQuestions.org. I thought this summed it up perfectly:

> What is the meaning of life? How can purpose, fulfillment, and satisfaction in life be found? How can something of lasting significance be achieved? So many people have never stopped to consider these important questions. They look back years later and wonder why their

relationships have fallen apart and why they feel so empty, even though they may have achieved what they set out to accomplish. An athlete who had reached the pinnacle of his sport was once asked what he wished someone would have told him when he first started playing his sport. He replied, "I wish that someone would have told me that when you reach the top, there's nothing there." Many goals reveal their emptiness only after years have been wasted in their pursuit. In our humanistic culture, people pursue many things, thinking that in them they will find meaning. Some of these pursuits include business success, wealth, good relationships, sex, entertainment, and doing good to others. People have testified that while they achieved their goals of wealth, relationships, and pleasure, there was still a deep void inside, a feeling of emptiness that nothing seemed to fill. The author of the biblical book of Ecclesiastes describes this feeling when he says, "Meaningless! Meaningless! …Utterly meaningless! Everything is meaningless." King Solomon, the writer of Ecclesiastes, had wealth far beyond measure, wisdom beyond any man of his time or ours, hundreds of women, palaces, gardens that were the envy of everyone, the best food and wine, and every form of entertainment available. He said at one point that anything his heart wanted, he pursued. And yet he summed up "life under the sun"—life lived as though all there is to life is what we can see with our eyes and experience with our senses—as meaningless. Why is there such a void? Because God created us for something beyond what we can experience in the here and now. Solomon said of God, "He has also set eternity in the hearts of men"

(Ecclesiastes 3:11). In our hearts, we are keenly aware that the "here and now" is not all that there is. (www.gotquestions.org)

Paul achieved all his dreams, studied under the best Jewish scholars, and was well-advanced in education. Yet, with all the accolades and remarkable achievements, Paul said,

> Yet indeed I also count all things loss for the excellence of the knowledge of Christ Jesus my Lord, for Whom I have suffered the loss of all things, and count them as rubbish, that I may gain Christ and be found in Him, not having my own righteousness, which is from the law, but that which is through faith in Christ, the righteousness which is from God by faith; that I may know Him and the power of His resurrection, and the fellowship of His sufferings, being conformed to His death, if, by any means, I may attain to the resurrection from the dead (Phil. 3:8–11).

Paul made it known throughout that his purpose in life was no longer of earthly concerns. Instead, he was called, chosen, and elected by God Himself, just as you and I still are today! He went on to say,

> Not that I have already attained, or am already perfected; but I press on, that I may lay hold of that for which Christ Jesus has also laid hold of me. Brethren, I do not count myself to have apprehended; but one thing I do, forgetting those things which are behind and reaching forward to those things which are ahead, I press toward the goal for the prize of the upward call of God in Christ Jesus. (Phil. 3:12–14)

What I've been writing about in this chapter are all things we have encountered over the course of our journey that have forced us to make difficult decisions that could never have been made without first knowing God through experiencing His divine providence and knowing His plan for our lives. Furthermore, we must learn how to be still and know that He is God and trust His faithfulness. God knows that none of this is easy; moreover, we know it's not easy. But we will also come to understand that life isn't easy, and without God, it's simply impossible! God is Creator and Master of the world as well as the Lord and Master of history. And through numerous events in history, God's Word has always been validated. His promises never fail. We call this "divine providence."

Think for a moment of a small child learning to swim for the very first time. I can still remember standing at the edge of the water at Timber Lake just east of Lathrop, Missouri, with my dad standing directly in front of me with his arms stretched out and ready to catch me the second I found the courage or faith to overcome my fears and jump. I knew in my heart, based on his words of assurance, that he would never let me drown, that this would work out for my good, and that in no time at all I would be the envy of the fish kingdom! But I still had to jump if I were ever going to learn how to exercise the genuineness of my faith in my dad's ability to catch me and uphold me if I started to sink!

That may be why Paul chose his famous words of humility that have touched so many lives throughout the ages, saying he had not attained or been perfected; but nevertheless, he pressed on that he may lay hold of that for which Christ Jesus had first laid hold of him. I can't even count the times I have had to turn to this powerful passage when I too found myself approaching swifter, more turbulent waters and needed to calm my spirit and strengthen my resolve, knowing that my Father in heaven would never turn His back on me or ever let me perish! Like Paul, I too forget those things that are behind me and reach forward toward those things still ahead. I too press on toward the goal for that unperishable prize of the upward call of God in Christ Jesus for my life (Phil. 3:12–14)! "Oh, the depth of the riches both of the wisdom and knowledge of God! How unsearchable are His judgments and His ways past finding out!" (Rom. 11:33).

Many people growing up in today's postmodern society pay thousands of dollars each year in their search for true love. I too have experienced the excruciating anxiety of feeling alone, abandoned, and unwanted. But on March 6, 1997, I personally encountered the compassion and concern of Jesus Christ, who said, "I love you, and I know your situation! Ellis, if you will just commit your ways to Me this day and trust Me, I will restore all the love that was taken from your life!"

As I mentioned before, I made the right choice that day and, like Job, the Lord has blessed these latter days far more than the beginning (Job 42:12)! And not only did He deliver on His promise to restore all the love that was taken from my life, but Peggi and I also testify that our God is indeed a good, good Father Who cares deeply for the needs of those who already know Him and love Him as well as the needs of fallen humanity. The Lord is not slow in keeping His promise, as some understand slowness. Instead He is patient with you, not wanting anyone to perish but wanting everyone to come to repentance (2 Pet. 3:9).

Peggi and I are both continually blown away by what is nothing short of a beautiful marriage that was joined together through the manifold wisdom of God for not only love but also for the fulfillment of His divine calling on both our lives! But again, we are the only ones empowered to make that decision regarding who and what it is that is worth abandoning everything we have and everything we ever hope to be for. Jesus said, "The thief comes only to steal and kill and destroy. I came that they may have life and have it abundantly" (John 10:10)!

I will close this chapter with a story Peggi and I heard while attending an evangelistic conference here in Colorado Springs. Erwin Lutzer, the well-known pastor of Moody Church in Chicago, Illinois, was the featured speaker for that night. Mr. Lutzer shared an unforgettable story. Although he had spoken metaphorically, his story gave a huge lift to our hearts regarding the cost of discipleship and the test of trusting the Word of God. He spoke of a poor beggar that was down to his last bowl of rice and on the brink of literal starvation. But one day, while walking beside a road, the poor beggar noticed an individual of royal decent, lavishly wealthy beyond imagination, being escorted down the road in his spectacular solid gold chariot that was elaborate beyond anything he had ever seen before in his lifetime. He was accompanied by other quite stunningly beautiful but less important chariots.

As he drew near the poor beggar, the beggar stopped his chariot and asked the wealthy man to bless him. But instead of responding in the manner that the poor beggar had demanded, the person of royalty asked the poor man to give him some of his rice. This angered the poor man, but, despite his poor emotional state, he gave the man a single grain of rice—though begrudgingly, knowing it was all he had left to survive on. He then asked the wealthy man a second time to bless him, and again, the person of royal decent asked the poor man to give him some of his rice. This caused an even greater degree of anger. But again, despite his growing frustration, the poor man again begrudgingly gave the wealthy man another single grain of his rice. He then asked the wealthy man a third time to bless him, and once again, the person of royal decent asked the poor beggar to give him a portion of his rice. This time the poor beggar was infuriated and angrily responded in what was an almost violent outburst, telling the wealthy man how this was the last grain of rice he would give him until the wealthy man blessed him in kind or at least to the same degree! The person of royal decent responded with, "Then I guess we're done here." As he was driving off, the poor beggar looked down into his bowl of rice and noticed three shiny pieces of gold, each the size of a single grain of rice. The poor beggar fell to his knees weeping, saying, "Oh, Lord, I wish I had given it all!"

The whole point in this chapter is to share with you the actual process God used to lift me up from that horrible pit of destruction that nearly cost me my life to living this remarkable life with my gorgeous wife, Peggi—a life that was paid for in full by Jesus Christ! We have learned the truth behind the message and reaped the blessing from Peggi's favorite verse, which says, "Those who sow in tears shall reap with joyful shouting. For he who goes to and fro weeping, carrying his bag of seed, shall indeed come again with a shout of joy, bringing his sheaves with him" (Ps. 126:5–6)! Amen!

We were all created with a God-shaped hole in the center of our hearts and souls that can only be satisfied through a personal relationship with Jesus Christ! Also, whoever sows sparingly should also expect to reap sparingly, and whoever sows bountifully will also reap bountifully. The same truth applies for love, money, grace, mercy, and faith—or anything that can be deposited as an investment toward a hope and future for someone else's life, as Christ has given so freely for us.

> Remember, God is able to make all grace abound to you so that, having all sufficiency in all things at all times, you may abound in every good work. As it is written, "He has distributed freely, He has given to the poor; His righteousness endures forever." He Who supplies seed to the sower and bread for food will supply and multiply your seed for sowing and increase the harvest of your righteousness. You will be enriched in every way to be generous in every way, which through us will produce thanksgiving to God. (2 Cor. 9:8–11)

So give, and it will be given to you. Good measure, pressed down, shaken together, and running over will be put into your bosom.

However, I have discovered that the best things in this life are seldom measured in gold pieces or paper money. And what God does give in exchange for our trust in Him—our generosity and love for Him and others and our obedience toward His word—you wouldn't trade for all the money in the world! But remember, with the same measure that you use it will be measured back to you (Luke 6:38). "Radical obedience to Christ is not easy," says Pastor David Platt. "It's not comfort, not health, not wealth, and not prosperity in this world. Radical obedience to Christ risks losing all these things. But in the end, such risk finds its reward in Christ. And He is more than enough for us" (David Platt from his book *Radical: Taking Back Your Faith from the American Dream*). "But indeed for this purpose I have raised you up, that I may show My power in you, and that My name may be declared in all the earth" (Exod. 9:16).

CHAPTER 8

IT IS NOT GOOD FOR MAN TO BE ALONE!

Peggi and I were married on Valentine's Day of 2009, and shortly thereafter, she began to share a vision with me that God had first shared with her—a vision that, quite frankly, was way over my head. And even after the amazing promises God had made to me and has since fulfilled, I simply could not comprehend the magnitude of this vision. Peggi, however, never once questioned God, knowing what He had already accomplished in and through my life, referring specifically to what took place on March 6, 1997, and beyond.

On the other hand, she and I both knew that God was preparing our hearts for a specific purpose that would involve me sharing my testimony. Neither of us knew how that would involve God raising up a two-state nonprofit organization or that we would both endure testing beyond anything either of us had ever experienced before. But again, as it is written: to whom much is given, from him much will be required; and to whom much has been committed, of him they will ask much more (Luke 12:48).

If God chooses to entrust someone with a special responsibility, we shouldn't be surprised when certain sacrifices and hardships are required of us. A life of much reward comes with much sacrifice and responsibility, because both people and God will demand the most of us. But certain religious leaders, on the other hand, will scrutinize every last move and decision we make—and not always with good intentions, which was the case in Luke chapter twelve. This entire portion of Scripture reveals much of what's on my heart that aroused the writing of this book. In fact, the whole idea behind the message of *Wanted* or the events we do is to assure those who feel left behind, excluded, of no value, or forgotten that God has not forgotten anyone. If that sounds like you, just know this: God is for you (Rom. 8:31)!

In Luke 14, Jesus makes this subject the foremost topic of discussion. He exposes deceitful hearts and turns an entire religious system upside down and inside out in the process. I use the term *discussion* loosely because this is a perfect example that demonstrates the depth of the riches of the wisdom and knowledge of God and shows just how unsearchable His judgments and His ways truly are beyond finding out (Rom. 11:33). He is the Master at using false teachers' own practices to tie their tongues and leave them speechless (reference John 8:1–11). And, in this case, the religious leaders were terrified of trying to cross-examine our mighty Lord and Savior, Jesus Christ, the Author and Master of both words and wisdom!

It all happened on a certain Sabbath when Jesus was invited to dine at the house of a ruler of the Pharisees. Jesus never turned down a dinner invitation from anyone, and sure enough, they were watching him carefully. At the ruler's home was a man before Jesus who had dropsy (congestive heart failure). Luke reports how Jesus responded to both the lawyers and the Pharisees, saying, "Is it lawful to heal on the Sabbath or not?" But they remained silent. And, in their defense, it would be foolish for anyone to try and match wits with God, in Whom are hidden all the treasures of wisdom and knowledge (Col. 2:3). So Jesus took the ill man, healed him, and sent him away. And He said to them, "Which of you, having a son or an ox that has fallen into a well on a Sabbath day, will not immediately pull him out?" And they could not reply to these things (Luke 14:2–6).

Now, you might be asking yourself, "What does this have to do with me being wanted?" Well, in reading on down a few verses to Luke 14:17–24, you will again see the difference between how man values certain members of society and how Jesus values the same people. It will further help put things into perspective regarding the demoniac from Mark 5 in the opening of the book!

The story begins with the words, "A man once gave a great banquet and invited many." The man in the parable, of course, is God!

> And at the time for the banquet he sent his servant to say to those who had been invited, "Come, for everything is now ready." But they all alike began to make excuses. The first said to him, "I have bought a field, and I must go out and see it. Please have me excused." And another said, "I have bought five yoke of oxen, and I go to examine them. Please have me excused." And another said, "I have married a wife, and therefore I cannot come." So the servant came and reported these things to his master. Then the master of the house became angry and said to his servant, "Go out quickly to the streets and lanes of the city, and bring in the poor, crippled, blind and the lame." And the servant said, "Sir, what you commanded has been done, and still there is room." And the master said to the servant, "Go out to the highways and hedges and compel people to come in, that my house may be filled. For I tell you, none of those men who were invited shall taste my banquet." (Luke 14:17–24)

Matthew adds additional details in Matthew 22. He says those originally invited paid no attention to the invitation. And please understand that this parable references the nation of Israel rejecting their Messiah and is by no means insinuating that any of us were somehow chosen by default without really being wanted. As far as Christians are concerned, we are all children of God through faith in Christ Jesus. For as many as were baptized into Christ have put on Christ. There is neither Jew nor Greek; there is neither slave nor free; there is neither male nor female, for you are all one in Christ Jesus (Gal. 3:26–28).

Our Father just happens to have a special heart for the physically, emotionally, and spiritually broken, and has a special purpose for each one. When I consider the demoniac and what God has done in my life—in addition to the lives of Dwight L. Moody, Pastor Raul Ries, Mike MacIntosh, Fanny Jane Crosby, and so many others (as well as the impact they have had on both my life and society)—it occurred to me that these courageous brothers and sisters of faith were not just wanted by God; they were, in fact, God's Most Wanted! Jesus spoke in yet another parable regarding how the Shepherd will leave behind the ninety-nine healthy sheep to seek that which is lost, the one who has strayed from the truth as well as the lush green pastures and still, calm serenity of God's Word and dwelling place (Matt. 18:12–Luke 15:4).

Now, I would like to clarify the meaning behind the phrase "God's Most Wanted." Essentially, what I'm saying is this: God knows those who are in serious danger emotionally and/or living in a volatile environment, vulnerable in their weakness and in dire need of His divine intervention. A fantastic book to help better understand this and other life's mysteries is *A Shephard Looks at Psalm 23* by Phillip Keller. In his book, Keller breaks down Psalm 23 into simple terms, explaining how sheep, by nature, are simply reckless and clumsy creatures that survive under the constant watch and tender care of the Shepherd. And amazingly, sheep recognize and will only respond to their Shepherd's voice.

Jesus said, "When the Good Shepherd brings out His own sheep, He goes before them; and the sheep follow Him, for they know His voice" (John 10:4). What does it mean when it says "He goes before them"? Jesus went before us in death and was raised again from the dead—only, unlike Lazarus and others in Scripture who were also raised from the dead, Jesus was the first to conquer death and hell once and for all, never experiencing death again. In addition, the Bible says, "Whom He did foreknow, He also did predestinate to be conformed to the image of His Son, that He might be the firstborn among many brethren" (Rom. 8:29).

> Christ is the head of the body, the church: Who is the beginning, the firstborn from the dead; that in all things He might have the preeminence. (Col. 1:18)
>
> Therefore, we are buried with Him by baptism into death: that like as Christ was raised up from the dead by the glory of the Father, even so we also should walk in newness of life. For if we have been planted together in the likeness of His death, we shall be also in the likeness of His resurrection. (Rom. 6:4–5)

Yet His true followers, those who were purchased by His blood (1 Pet. 1:19) and belong to Him, will by no means follow a stranger, but will flee from him, for they do not know the voice of strangers (John 10:4–5). "'I am the good Shepherd,' says Jesus. 'The good Shepherd gives His life for the sheep'" (John 10:11). A sheep must be pretty special in the eyes of the Shepherd for Him to give His own life to save a simple-minded, smelly creature like that, but that's exactly what Jesus Christ did for all of us on the cross at Mount Calvary! But in order to inherit the manifold blessing of God, we must know our Shepherd's voice, pick up our own crosses, and follow Him (Luke 9:23). Again, Jesus said, "My sheep hear My voice, and I know them, and they follow Me" (John 10:27).

> Put on then, as God's chosen ones, holy and beloved, compassionate hearts, kindness, humility, meekness, and patience, bearing with one another and, if one has a complaint against another, forgiving each other; as the Lord has forgiven you, so you also must forgive. And above all these put on love, which binds everything together in perfect harmony. And let the peace of Christ rule in your hearts, to which indeed you were called in one body. And be thankful. Let the Word of Christ dwell in you richly, teaching and

> admonishing one another in all wisdom, sing-
> ing psalms and hymns and spiritual songs, with
> thankfulness in your hearts to God. And what-
> ever you do, in word or deed, do everything in
> the name of the Lord Jesus, giving thanks to God
> the Father through Him. (Col. 3:12–17)!

Jesus is the Good Shepherd, and those who call on Him for salvation are His sheep! The parallel is that we also survive, thrive, and reign in great victory over Satan and tragic circumstances by the constant watch and tender mercies of our Great God and Shepherd, Jesus Christ, Who promised He would never leave us or forsake us for any reason. "'Have I not commanded you?' says the Lord, 'Be strong and of good courage; do not be afraid, nor be dismayed, for the Lord your God is with you wherever you go'" (Josh. 1:9).

Keller also pointed out how, if a sheep were to stumble and end up on its back, it would have no ability to turn itself upright, making it easy prey without help and protection from its Shepherd. We are instructed to humble ourselves beneath the mighty hand of God so that at the proper time He may exalt us, casting all our anxieties on Him, knowing how much He cares for us. Peter said,

> Be sober-minded and watchful. Your adver-
> sary the devil prowls around like a roaring lion,
> seeking someone to devour. Resist him, firm in
> your faith, knowing that the same kinds of suffer-
> ing are being experienced by your brotherhood
> throughout the world. And after you have suf-
> fered a little while, the God of all grace, Who
> has called you to His eternal glory in Christ, will
> Himself restore, confirm, strengthen, and estab-
> lish you. (1 Pet. 5:6–10)

Keller's amazing book, based on his firsthand experience of rais-
ing and working with sheep, is paired with his extensive knowledge of God's Word. Keller's thesis is notable, due to the fact that we, by

nature, tend to fight and wrestle with God when He is pursuing us, and, for whatever reasons, we resist His saving grace and ignorantly take Satan's bait. Yet in His infinite knowledge of time, space, and eternity, and being motivated by an infinite love so strong that He chose to give His life to save ours, He—Jesus, the Good Shephard—will often break a limb if that's what it takes to redeem our lives and souls!

You may have seen the portrait of Jesus carrying a lamb over His shoulders. That is a genuine reality regarding how far our Dear Lord will go to bring us back (or for the first time) into the fold. Additionally, although undoubtedly a last resort, God loves us so much that He would rather disable us temporarily in this life than let us perish for eternity! In essence, not all suffering is a result of someone wanting to do us harm!

We should live every day as though the Lord were coming back today! But beware, cautions Peter, who said,

> Dear friends, this is now my second letter to you. I have written both of them as reminders to stimulate you to wholesome thinking. I want you to recall the words spoken in the past by the holy prophets and the command given by our Lord and Savior through your apostles. Above all, you must understand that in the last days scoffers will come, scoffing and following their own evil desires. They will say, "Where is this 'coming' He promised? Ever since our ancestors died, everything goes on as it has since the beginning of creation." (2 Pet. 3:1–4)
>
> But do not forget this one thing, dear friends: With the Lord a day is like a thousand years, and a thousand years are like a day. The Lord is not slow in keeping His promise, as some understand slowness. Instead He is patient with you, not wanting anyone to perish, but everyone to come to repentance. But the day of the Lord

will come like a thief in the night. The heavens will disappear with a roar; the elements will be destroyed by fire, and the earth and everything done in it will be laid bare. (2 Pet. 2:8–10)

Tragically, at the Lord's first advent, His people were not prepared, and in what amounted to unbelief, our Lord was rejected and crucified by the very people He came to save.

John 1:11 says that He came to that which was His own (His world, His creation, His possession) and to those who were His own, the Jewish nation, as He was of the lineage of David, from the tribe of Judah, the house of Benjamin, etc. However, the Jewish nation did not receive or welcome Him! Matthew says they ignored Jesus and went off, one to his farm, another to his business, while the rest seized His servants, treated them shamefully, and killed them. The king (God) was angry, and he sent his troops and destroyed those murderers and burned their city (a foreshadowing of what later happened in 70 AD). Then he said to his servants, "The wedding feast is ready, but those invited were not worthy. Go therefore to the main roads and invite to the wedding feast as many as you find" (Matt. 22:5–9). Jesus wrapped up the parable by saying that many are called, but few are chosen (vs. 14).

Luke chapter fourteen has become the blueprint for His Heart United Ministries. Rest assured, God knows exactly what it will take to prepare His children for the journey He has arranged for each of us. It will humble us, and it will test us. It could also be considered as a time of training and is imperative for our own benefit! It is the difference between being a hearer of the Word and being an effectual doer of the Word—obedience versus rebellion; believer or nonbeliever. Moreover, it is the difference between life and death!

Therefore whoever hears these sayings of Mine, and does them, I will liken him to a wise man who built his house on the rock: and the rain descended, the floods came, and the winds blew and beat on that house; and it did not fall,

for it was founded on the rock. But everyone
who hears these sayings of Mine, and does not
do them, will be like a foolish man who built
his house on the sand: and the rain descended,
the floods came, and the winds blew and beat
on that house; and it fell. And great was its fall.
(Matt. 7:24–27)

We have made it our focus to go out to the streets and lanes
in our city and anywhere a door opens to us, in addition to seeking
out the highways, hedges, back roads, jails, city parks, churches, and
anywhere else we can go to find the poor, blind, and lame. We seek
out as many of them as we can find, letting those who are desperate
know that they have a Father in heaven Who loves them more than
life itself, and that they are not only wanted by Him and others, but
that God also has a plan for their lives no matter what their past or
present situation may be!

Had it not been for God's immeasurable love for me, I would not
have been delivered from drugs and alcohol. I would not have been
delivered from prison. I would not know Peggi Sue Lucas. And had
I never met and had the opportunity to join her for an October 25,
2008, ministry event in St Joseph, Missouri, there would undoubtedly be no His Heart United Network of Christian Ministries that
shares our vision for the lost, broken, and hurting people of our frac-
tured generation. There would be no *Potter and the Clay* or *Wanted*
books. There would be no Ellis Lucas original songs recorded or the
lives God has touched through knowing our story and the ministry
He established as a result of the wonderful things He has done in our
lives!

Nevertheless, as wonderful as our lives in Jesus have become,
there is only one appropriate way to conclude this chapter. I want to
share a brief testimony of one of Peggi's and my all-time heroes of the
faith, Joni Eareckson Tada. As a teenager, Joni loved life. She loved
riding horses, swimming, etc. But in 1967, while swimming with
friends, Joni dove into a lake not knowing that the water was shallow.
She broke her neck, paralyzing her body from the neck down and

leaving her a quadriplegic. She would be confined to a wheelchair for the rest of her natural life. For the next two years during her rehabilitation, Joni struggled. She struggled with life, with God, and with her paralysis.

Today, however, Joni is an internationally known mouth artist, creating some of the most magnificent works of art the world has ever seen. Her art has inspired other quadriplegics to not just adapt to their brokenness but to rewrite the way life is performed, demonstrating how nothing is impossible with God! Remarkable brothers and sisters in Jesus such as Ron Heagy, who also was injured in a swimming accident and paralyzed from the neck down, found himself with similar emotions to Joni. Like her, Ron struggled with life, with God, with his paralysis, and admittedly wished he had died in the accident.

But God had other plans. Ron was a gifted athlete before his accident, a man who was born with the heart of a lion—a heart that served him well in that it wouldn't allow him to give up. That became his creed, his message to the world: "Never Give Up!" He was given an unshakable faith to conquer the mountain of impossibilities, defying the odds and becoming an iconic mouth artist in his own right. Ron Heagy, like Joni Eareckson Toda, is an absolutely astonishing human being and man of faith in Christ Jesus.

Peggi and I met Ron while attending a Joni and Friends event here in Colorado Springs with our dear friend and sister in Christ Kelly Jean Leggett. We were stunned by what we witnessed as a result of what God has created from the shattered pieces of this amazing man's life. In addition, Joni is a talented vocalist, a radio host, an author of seventeen books, and an advocate for disabled persons worldwide. Her story is all the proof you'll ever need to see and understand why you should never accept failure, isolation, loneliness, singleness, etc., nor entertain the thought of seeing yourself as damaged beyond repair!

Joni has proved that if we present our bodies—quadriplegic or not—a living sacrifice, holy, acceptable to God, which is our reasonable service, and be transformed by the renewing of our minds, we will indeed prove what is that good and acceptable and perfect will of

God for both our lives and the sake of others through our example of faith (Rom. 12:1–2)! What's more, because of the commitment and trust Joni has placed in her precious Lord and Savior Jesus, God has also granted Joni the sweetest desires of her life: her beloved husband Ken Tada. In 1982, Joni was married to her amazing husband, Ken. Ken retired from thirty-two years of teaching in 2004, and now ministers full-time alongside Joni as they travel across the country and around the world.

I have included a short list of spiritual markers at the end of this chapter commemorating each milestone along Joni's journey. And in the closing of chapter eight, I will just say that I hope you took notice of the title for this chapter: "It Is Not Good for Man to Be Alone!" Joni is not only a remarkable human being, but she is also the completion of her husband, Ken, whose life would have never been what it is today without the help of his beloved and ever-so-special, one-of-a-kind helpmate, Joni Eareckson Tada.

Then the Lord God said, "It is not good that the man should be alone; I will make him a helper fit for him" (Gen. 2:18)! I say, "Go, Joni, go!" Amen! For more information on Joni and Ken, visit their website at: www.joniandfriends.org. Or for more information on Ron Heagy, visit his website at www.ronheagy.com.

- 1974 - Joni's appearance on *The Today Show* opens a new door to national exposure.
- 1976 - The first edition of the *Joni* book is released. It will eventually be translated into more than forty-five languages resulting in over four million copies in print.
- 1979 - The Joni movie is released. It's shown around the world, resulting in over 250,000 decisions for Christ.
- 1979 - Joni and Friends is established to address the needs of families affected by disability after the *Joni* book and movie generate an outpouring of response. Joni and a small but dedicated staff begin the work from a two-room office in California.
- 1982 - Joni begins recording her Joni and Friends radio program.

- 1988 - President Ronald Reagan appoints Joni to the National Council on Disability. Joni advocates for the passage of the Americans with Disabilities Act.
- 1990 - Joni attends the signing of the Americans with Disabilities Act at the White House.
- 1991 - After attending a Family Conference sponsored by the federal government and National Council on Disability, Joni challenged the ministry to do better. The first Family Retreat was held in Cannon Beach, Oregon.
- 1994 - Wheels for the World was founded, with the first wheelchair delivered in Ghana.
- 1997 - The Joni and Friends International Disability Center opens its doors.
- 2004 - International Family Retreats begin.
- 2007 - Christian Institute on Disability is founded.
- 2014 - 100,000th wheelchair delivered by Wheels for the World in Ghana.
- 2017 - Joni celebrates fifty years of God's faithfulness to her in her wheelchair.

"Trust in the Lord, and do good; dwell in the land, and feed on His faithfulness. Delight yourself also in the Lord, and He shall give you the desires of your heart" (Ps. 37:3–4)! Amen!

CHAPTER 9

FAITH WITHOUT WORKS IS DEAD

Undoubtedly, the memories of my mother's persistent Christ-centered devotion lived out in her daily life left an indelible impression on my heart that remained deeply embedded in my sub-conscious long after she was gone. Those memories somehow man-aged to transcend life and death, seasons of joy and seasons of pain, countless trials and unbearably difficult circumstances that left me spiritually, emotionally, financially, and relationally crippled with mental paralysis that, in my mind, would simply be impossible to overcome. Every detail of my life before Christ led me to believe that hope was irredeemable!

"Yet in all these things," says the Apostle Paul, "we are more than conquerors through Him Who loved us. For I am persuaded that neither death nor life, nor angels nor principalities nor powers, nor things present nor things to come, nor height nor depth, nor any other created thing, shall be able to separate us from the love of God which is in Christ Jesus our Lord" (Rom. 8:37–39)!

Trials and tribulations are essential not only for enhancing our confidence in our ability to handle God's calling, but also so that we may learn to rest in the knowledge of His sovereign control over all things at all times. Then when perilous times do come and storm clouds gather, we can be confident that no weapon formed against us will ever prosper (Isa. 54:17). Some of us, though, are fully aware that many of the trials we have endured are self-inflicted hardships brought on by our own rebellion. And although we know our own faults and failures, wickedness is a shared and relentless foe that affects all human beings. In fact, "Suffering has been stronger than all other teaching," says Charles Dickens. He also noted that suffering had taught him to understand what his heart used to be, saying, "I have been bent and broken, but I always hope into a better shape."

The amazing Elisabeth Elliot said, "I am not a theologian or a scholar, but I am very aware of the fact that pain is necessary to all of us. In my own life, I think I can honestly say that out of the deepest pain has come the strongest conviction of the presence of God and the love of God." One thing I tell people regarding past sins and present guilt is that there is value in the lessons we learned even in our sin! Suffering should be our greatest teacher, because once we see the benefits in the buffeting, only then can we truly appreciate the value of the cross and the suffering Jesus Christ endured on our behalf!

Jonathan Edwards once said that the only thing we contributed to our salvation was the sin that made it necessary! I have said on occasions that had I not experienced the pain and suffering of my life before I knew Jesus Christ and was saved, there would be no His Heart United Network, nor would I be the person I am today doing what I absolutely love doing. "Therefore, even in this," says the Apostle Peter, "we greatly rejoice, even though now for a little while, if necessary, we have been distressed by various trials, so that the proof of our faith, being more precious than gold which is perishable, even though tested by fire, may be found to result in praise and glory and honor at the revelation of Jesus Christ" (1 Pet. 1:6–7)!

Let us prove ourselves doers of the Word and not merely hearers (James 1:22)! In other words, it's time to stop wasting our lives looking for the key to happiness! The door is open, unlocked, and waiting, but only you can make the bold decision to stand up, look up, and walk through. "Ask, and it will be given to you; seek, and you will find; knock, and it will be opened to you. For everyone who asks receives, and he who seeks finds, and to him who knocks it will be opened" (Matt. 7:7–8)! Furthermore, these temporary light afflictions that are producing for us a glorious eternal weight in glory (2 Cor. 4:17) are also distinguishing between the many who are called and the few who are actually chosen (Matt. 22:14).

Nevertheless, being called, chosen, and entrusted with a special responsibility should never be taken lightly, regardless if it is wonderful in every way—especially when Jesus Christ redeems the irredeemable, restores the unrestorable, and unashamedly wants the unwanted. The things that were so despised by all, He crowned with glory and honor! Beware of your own motives, "For no other foundation can anyone lay than that which is laid, which is Jesus Christ," says the Apostle Paul. "And if anyone builds on this foundation with gold, silver, precious stones, wood, hay, or straw, each one's work will become clear; for the Day will declare it, because it will be revealed by fire; and the fire will test each one's work, of what sort it is." Paul continues by saying that if anyone's work which he has built on it endures, he will receive a reward. "But if anyone's work is burned, he will suffer loss; though he himself will be saved, yet so as through fire" (1 Cor. 3:11–15). The point is this, friends: faith without works is dead (James 2:17)!

Peggi and I both knew that God had ordained our marriage for numerous reasons including companionship and, as in any case, a beautiful love relationship. But our marriage was also intended as a union for the cause of Jesus Christ! Peggi really is the sunshine of my life and my best friend forever, and as I mentioned in the previous chapter but not in these words, Peggi has brought focus, determination, passion, and nearly everything under the sun that God uses to keep me pressing in and pressing on toward the goal for the prize of the upward call of Christ Jesus on both our lives. But above all that, a three-cord strand is not easily—and most often is never—broken (Eccles. 4:12).

Jesus Christ represents the third strand in the cord and the superglue that holds it all bound and fitted together! Furthermore, our union has been a remarkable journey that I wouldn't trade for all the money in the world! Nonetheless, I must confess, it hasn't always been easy discerning the pathway or being obedient to the mission. And one thing I can testify regarding our journey is how there were many tears shed when we decided to pack up everything we owned and set out on this journey that had no other guarantees than what the Spirit of the Lord was speaking to our spirits, along with the living Word of God affirming and confirming that we were indeed doing the right thing!

I had just completed a seven-year season of preparation that not only included leading worship and preparing our church family for receiving God's Word at Liberty, Missouri, but also preparing the message and presenting the Word myself. And by all accounts, it appeared that God was preparing me for becoming a pastor. But during that time I was never settled and, in fact, was quite restless. Likewise, I began to question my calling as it became evident to me that my heart's desire, talents, and spiritual gifts were not necessarily geared toward becoming a full-time staff pastor but rather were geared more toward evangelistic outreach, reaching the lost, and assisting with the restoration of broken lives.

I always felt closest to God and most alive when doors would open for the Dry Bones Band, a little band formed by two close friends and myself for what started out as just three great friends having the time of our lives visiting churches, community centers, city parks, etc., and sharing testimonies, presenting the gospel, and inviting people to respond to the invitation to know Jesus Christ. But lo and behold, that season was nearing its end, and Peggi and I were about to embark on a new seven-year journey that would begin with severe difficulties and testing that I would not have survived without the strength and immovable faith of my beloved wife. There again, faith without works is dead, but where faith is alive and empowered, nothing is impossible for those who are in Christ Jesus!

I quickly came to appreciate what the Lord meant when He said, "It is not good for the man to be alone. I will make a helper who is just right for him" (Gen. 2:18)! Where I am weak, Peggi is strong and mighty! She has been a woman of tremendous faith in God ever since she was a little girl growing up in a tiny town in Northeast Iowa. But in all honesty, leaving Missouri and all we had behind was a giant and never before attempted step of faith for us both! Leaving the Dry Bones Band was one of the most difficult decisions I have ever had to make. And when I sat down with Peggi and her best friend, Rhonda Schram, the night before we left town, I honestly think dying may have been easier than feeling the pain of those two precious and godly best friends' hearts being torn to pieces and watching that river of tears flowing down both their sad faces. Rhonda is a dear friend and anointed sister in Jesus who predicted very specific details regarding Peggi's future husband and marriage prior to us ever meeting. And when God did begin to move, it all fell into place exactly as she had predicted! But nevertheless, we both knew our future was not in Missouri!

I will never forget my last day at work for Estes Express Lines in Missouri. I felt overwhelmed with anxiety, wondering if we were doing the right thing and praying that God would calm my heart if moving west truly was His plan and His will for our lives. Sure enough, I don't recall a time where God had made anything any clearer than He did to us that day!

We were scheduled to do a weekend evangelistic outreach in South Dakota later that year featuring the band, Bread of Stone, who was also our production company for the weekend. However, I had never met them before. And while on my final run for Estes, I was delivering to a small rural school located in Dearborn, Missouri. As I arrived, I passed a large green tour bus parked in the back parking lot near the rear entrance of the school gymnasium. I got out to begin my delivery and was stunned at the sight of tour cases scattered all over the parking lot with the name Bread of Stone on them. I quickly went inside the gymnasium and found the band and some family members, and I knew God had just answered my prayer. I called Peggi, who was still a half hour north, to tell her what had just happened, and as we were talking, I noticed the most beautiful rainbow I had ever seen. It was a crystal-clear day in Northwest Missouri with no rain in sight. I started to tell Peggi about that beautiful rainbow, but to my surprise she was looking at the same one.

Both of us immediately thought about God's covenant promise to Noah—how He would never again bring destruction upon the whole earth by way of water. God hung the most magnificent rainbow overhead as a sign of peace that we were on the road that lead to abundant life and would no longer have to worry about a hope and future and could rule out a coming destruction by way of presumptuous decision making. God was leading us and confirmed His favor far above and beyond any reasonable doubt!

There were no financial or economic reasons for uprooting and leaving our jobs, friends, families, and church. What's more, most people thought our plans were ludicrous and foolish. However, and in their defense, I would have thought the same thing had I been in their shoes!

Abraham may have wrestled with the same issues when the Lord instructed him to "Get out of your country, from your family and from your father's house, to a land that I will show you" (Gen. 12:1b). God promised to make Abraham a great nation. He said He would bless him and make his name great, and that he would be a blessing to many (Gen. 12:2). Not once did unbelief ever cause him to waver concerning the promises God had made. Instead, Abraham grew strong in his faith as he gave glory to God, fully convinced that God was more than able to fulfill all that He had promised, exceedingly, abundantly above and beyond. That is why his faith was counted to him as righteousness (Rom. 4:20–22).

Peggi and I have always believed that faith is the substance of things hoped for, the evidence of things not seen (Heb. 11:1). And without faith, it is impossible to please God (Heb. 11:6). Our desire was to go west to a land that God would show us, believing that if we stood firm as Scripture had promised, we would win the souls we were brought here to reach (Luke 21:19), persevering through it all, rejoicing in hope, enduring tribulation patiently, and above all, continuing steadfastly in prayer (Rom. 12:12)!

Perseverance is defined as a course of action, a purpose, and a state of being, especially despite difficulties, obstacles, or discouragement. Neither Peggi nor I have wavered in our faith regarding what God had promised to us. He said, "My purpose will be established, and I will accomplish all My good pleasure" (Isa. 46:10). But again, faith without works is dead, and without faith it is impossible to please God (Heb. 11:6)!

Like Abraham, our faith grew strong and our hope began to come alive. Then in 2010, we were introduced to two precious identical twin brothers from Birmingham, Alabama—Rick and Mick

Vigneulle. And what we witnessed during our time with those two unique individuals was the hand of God at work in and through these brothers in ways we had never imagined. God was at work both in and through Rick and Mick's lives to will and to do for His good pleasure, reaching hundreds of high school and middle school aged kids here in America and around the world with the Gospel every time the door opened for a school assembly.

But in getting to know the twins on a very personal level, we were shocked to learn that during their adolescent and teenage years, both Rick and Mick were ADHD. They had learning disabilities and were not the prototypical guys you might expect to win hundreds of thousands of school-age kids to Jesus Christ. It was like having a Billy Graham cut into two mini Grahams with the mission to reach the next generation of believers for Jesus Christ!

Rick opened up to me about how he had wrestled with and resisted God's calling for two years due to feeling absolutely destitute of any confidence in his ability to live out that calling. But during that time, he began having dreams—once in which he was speaking before huge crowds of people—and became very confused about what the dreams meant, so he began to pray for God to help him with his heart and his willingness. He believed that God was calling both he and Mick to serve as youth pastors, and both were each called on by five different churches to interview for their vacant youth pastor positions.

Rick and Mick are both five feet, two inches tall and were both oblivious to the unthinkable God-given gifts and talents they were born with. Eventually they attended and graduated Liberty University and landed jobs working for Dr. Jerry Falwell in Lynchburg, Virginia. But like me, they were still unsettled and ever restless, sensing God had something more for them on the horizon. And sure enough, they were called by Light Ministries, which was located on the opposite end of the U.S. in California.

Unfortunately, six months later they were informed that Light Ministries was moving to Lynchburg, Virginia, where they had just moved from and, for whatever reason, felt as though God was telling them to stay in California. That drove them to their knees in search of hard answers, which led to an open door with none other than Tim LaHaye, a well-known Christian author and speaker who took them under his wing. This connection led to Dr. David Jeremiah giving them a slot on his national television show. That opened even more doors, as they were invited by Pastors Adrian Rogers and Charles Stanley to appear on their television shows.

Then, while Rick was visiting a church one Sunday, he discovered he was an hour and a half late for Sunday school class. Feeling embarrassed, he decided to take a little detour through the library to avoid being noticed by anyone. But even there he couldn't outrun fate. In the library, he bumped into a gentleman named Tim Laycock. The two men made eye contact, undoubtedly sensing something peculiar about one another, and decided to introduce themselves.

Tim greeted Rick, and Rick said, "Pleased to meet you. My name is Rick."

Tim asked, "Are you Rick as in 'Rick and Mick'?"

And, being quite unknown at the time, Rick responded with surprise, "Yes, how did you know that?"

Tim answered by telling Rick that he had seen them on TV and that they were the ones he had come to see. Tim invited them to speak at a youth camp located in Arizona, and they were both ecstatic, saying that it had been their prayer to speak at youth camps and conferences.

After the camp concluded, some time had lapsed, and out of the blue they received another call from Tim asking them to once again join him for another youth outreach, which they assumed was another youth camp. To their surprise, Tim had moved his operation to Loveland, Colorado, and when they asked what camp they would be speaking at, they were utterly shocked to hear that they would not be speaking at a youth camp but were instead booked at—and would be speaking for—six public school assemblies. They were forbidden to talk about God and religion, and were instructed "by all means, whatever you do" not to mention the name of Jesus in any of the six assemblies.

Rick and Mick said they couldn't do that, stating that they were called to evangelize the young and reach the next generation of kingdom servants for Jesus Christ! But again, faith without works is dead, and without faith it is impossible to please God! In protest, the brothers said, "Even if we were to do something like that, we don't have any materials prepared or the right kind of music to play in that type of setting."

Tim responded by saying, "I understand that, and that's why I am giving you two weeks to get ready. But, guys, you have to do these assemblies because you are already committed and it would be a disaster to not show up now."

At the end of the week, Rick and Mick invited all the schools to a neutral location at a venue that could seat seven hundred people. They had prayed for at least two hundred kids to show up so there wouldn't be an empty auditorium, but to their surprise the building was full, and since the event wasn't sanctioned by a public school, Rick and Mick unloaded with the gospel. As a result, over a hundred kids were saved. And, as they say, the rest is history!

We learned so much from these two wonderful servants of the Lord who not only treat us like a part of their family but also introduced us to a whole new level of faith and understanding regarding evangelism and the Spirit of the Lord. I had never seen anything like it before and often wondered, "What is with all these kids? Why are all these young people so hungry for and open to receiving the Gospel when the rest of the public school system is vehemently opposed to the gospel or Jesus having a place in the most sacred of all places—the place where our kids go to be prepared for life and adulthood?" And to this day, after watching and participating firsthand, I honestly don't know the answer, but I do know what Jesus said: "Let the little children come to Me, and do not forbid them; for of such is the kingdom of heaven" (Matt. 19:14)!

There have been times when an entire school would break out into revival, but without faith, none of this would have—or ever could have—happened. Rick and Mick responding to their hearts' convictions has proven to be one of the greatest examples of where man's unapologetic faith and God's providence and approval integrate.

Rick and Mick would never write this story about themselves. What's more, apart from the help of a visual interpreter, they wouldn't even be able to write a story like this. Why? Because they are unable to see the beauty in the details of their own extraordinary lives due to the protective lenses of genuine humility that have been permanently placed before their eyes.

In fact, Rick and Mick have said numerous times, "We have never gotten over how or why God would use us! We flunked speech in high school because we were afraid to get up in front of our peers. We tell people now, 'God will use your inadequacies greater than He'll ever use your abilities, but you have to give Him your life.' We weren't spiritual giants either! We struggled with the same temptations everyone else did! But during this past month of ministry (fall of 2012), over five hundred more decisions were made for our mighty Jesus. Hallelujah!"

That is why I am honored to be able tell their story as it should be told. Why? Because Peggi and I were two of those lives! Rick and Mick invited us to join them on a South Dakota and Wyoming tour where we saw hundreds of middle and high school kids commit their young lives to knowing Christ and making Him known.

This dynamic duo are now internationally known youth evangelists as well as stellar comedians and contemporary music artists. Over the course of their ministry journey, they have served in all fifty states as well as fifteen countries around the world. They have been featured on *America's Funniest People*, conducted several chapel services for professional baseball teams including the Atlanta Braves, the Houston Astros, and the Los Angeles Dodgers, and have performed at 1600 Pennsylvania Ave, Washington, DC, home of the president of the United States and the epic center of the United States of America, the White House. They have been seen on *60 Minutes* and in *LIFE Magazine's 20th Century Highlight* book.

Rick and Mick have been favorites in hundreds of high school assemblies where they present their highly acclaimed program, "Attitude Check." Hundreds of thousands of school kids have made decisions for Jesus Christ because of this outstanding program. This worldwide evangelistic outreach was responsible for over fifteen thousand combined student and adult decisions for Jesus Christ in just two years alone! Their mission has always been to seek the lost of all ages and compel believers and nonbelievers alike to pursue knowing God's love, freedom, and hope.

Rick and Mick also never pass up an opportunity to challenge the people they come in contact with to be bold and unashamed witnesses before this lost and hurting generation, while sharing their joy-filled relationship with Jesus Christ with everyone they meet. They are committed to reaching our youth, their families, and adults alike with the everlasting, life-saving truth of Jesus Christ by providing culturally relevant and innovative programs in both schools and churches.

"Our desire," say Rick and Mick, "is to expand our influence by recruiting dynamic young talent for the purpose of sharing the Gospel, and providing a platform for reaching our nation's future Christian posterity through discipleship and equipping servant-minded, Christ-centered believers for effective worldwide ministry." But perhaps the greatest gift that God ever bestowed upon these two giants of the faith is the one that will always leave an indelible impression on the hearts they meet along their sojourn through this life—a contagious love for Jesus Christ and people.

It was never their ability to make people burst into laughter that caused so many people from all walks of life to fall in love with Jesus Christ; it was Christ in them supplying them with the ability to be a genuine reflection of His transparent heart, humility, and infinite love toward all people. It was love that conquered death and gave sight to the blind, and it was love that made these two special brothers from Birmingham, Alabama, irresistible and useful in reaching countless lost souls from around the world with the Gospel. "To Him Who is able to do far more abundantly beyond all that we ask or think, according to the power that works within us, to Him be the glory in the church and in Christ Jesus to all generations forever and ever" (Eph. 3:20–21). Amen!

I will conclude this chapter with these thoughts: Charles Haddon Spurgeon once said, "Friendship is one of the sweetest joys of life. Many might have failed beneath the bitterness of their trial had they not found a friend." No truer words on this subject have ever been spoken. "May He grant you according to your heart's desire and fulfill all your purpose. We will rejoice in your salvation, and in the name of our God we will set up our banners! May the Lord fulfill all your petitions" (Ps. 20:4–5). Amen!

CHAPTER 10

IDENTITY CRISIS

One of the first and more difficult challenges I encountered after becoming a Christian was trying to discern what was happening in my life after receiving Jesus Christ. The second challenge was me questioning why. Like Joni Eareckson Toda, I too had to learn life all over again. Also like Joni, the first two years were undoubtedly the most painful. Yet for me, they were also the most spectacular years of my life. The stress from all the rapid changes taking place in my life—as well as the literal transformation that accrued in my heart, spirit, and soul—was so intense that, at times, I wasn't sure I would survive long enough to know what happened or why. But not only did I survive—I now also overwhelmingly cherish the memories of those unforgettable days in the most violent spiritual conflict imaginable that was being waged over my soul.

It was during that time when God became more to me than just another storybook hero passed down from generation to generation. Instead of being another white-hat hero in another good-versus-evil story who always comes out on top in the end, God quickly became more real to me than the air I breathe. What was taking place during a good portion of those first two years as a Christian was nothing short of terrifying for a new believer who had zero understanding of a very real and awesome God at work in my life.

I wouldn't change a thing though now because of the priceless knowledge I gained during that time—especially in learning about the true nature and heart of God. He taught me how to trust His motives and sincerity and to never fear life's constant storms. He also removed any doubts I had regarding the legitimacy of who He is, who He has always been, or the thoughts He has always had toward me. That was a huge hurdle, since the years of pain and paranoia all but eradicated my ability to trust. Moreover, it took several years for the dark clouds to lift. God has undoubtedly awakened my understanding to knowing that He is and has always been for me, and that He is a good, good Father Who both knows and wants the very best for me.

Likewise, I am now confident and sure that whatever we encounter in this life as Christians, it will always be filtered through the impenetrable shield of God's sovereign grace and protection before it is ever allowed access into our lives. Although sadly, I also learned that humanity doesn't always feel the same way toward Him as He does and always will toward them. God's love in Christ Jesus is immutable; it will never change. The deception, however, is both blinding and heartbreaking, especially knowing the pain He still incurs from the rejection of His people even today and, moreover, the consequences they will face if they don't repent and return while there's still time.

"He will come with His mighty angels, in flaming fire," says the Apostle Paul, "bringing judgment on those who don't know God and on those who refuse to obey the Good News of our Lord Jesus. They will be punished with eternal destruction, forever separated from the Lord and from His glorious power" (2 Thess. 1:7–9)!

After my unexpected conversion to Christianity, I could see how God intentionally used the events of March 6, 1997, to plant the seeds for a life geared toward evangelism and sharing my story. During that time, God revealed to me what the fate of many well-intending people would look like: Many wonderful people would lose the race despite fearing God and knowing the truth, having always intended to get their hearts right with God. But day after day, year in and year out, they egregiously ignore God's plea for them to repent of their sin and turn to Jesus Christ for salvation. They keep procrastinating, taking life and God for granted, deceived into believing there will be a right time.

It is like the timeless proverbial warnings: the road to hell is paved with good intentions, and no good deed goes unpunished. Those following this path will find themselves devastated when they discover that time has suddenly and unexpectedly expired and they are separated from God forever. Like those people, I too heard that inner voice of God—not saying, but shouting, "Now is the acceptable time. Today is the day of salvation. Trouble is coming. Come back to Me now while you still can."

Like them, I too ignored the warning signs, procrastinated one day too long, and discovered it is a fearful and dreadful thing to fall into the hands of the living God [incurring His judgment and wrath]" (Heb. 10:31, AMP)! While foolishly risking my life and freedom in exchange for a few restless nights of shelter at a known meth house in Gladstone, Missouri, I rolled the dice betting that all would be all right! All I needed was two weeks to once again say that I cheated fate! But it wasn't meant to be. Each day the voice got louder and louder, and I knew something terrifying was about to happen.

I drove a truck by night, and each morning my intentions were to pack my belongings which could fit into a single suitcase and run for my life. But each day I would arrive exhausted and would tell myself, "Just one more day of rest, and tomorrow I am leaving for sure." Then finally on the sixth day, when I was ready and couldn't wait to pack up and leave while I still could, my life was forever changed. Unfortunately, time had expired and judgment had come! Shortly after I arrived, the North Kansas City SWAT Team raided the house and, in a brief moment, my life was gone!

Isaiah said, "The name of the Lord will be feared from the west, and His glory from the rising of the sun." I have always known that what God did in my life beyond that point was not all for my benefit, but was meant to demonstrate His divine power and providence to say to a world of wayward sinners, "I love you, and I'm here for you! I know your situation, and no matter what your present situation in this life may be, I can help! Nothing is impossible for Me!"

His infinite attributes have been made known before a lost and hurting world through the great work He has done in my life. But heaven knows, I had no idea there would be another day or that God would wipe away every crumb of evidence and every fingerprint as though I had never been in that house. Just as He promises to remove our sins as far as the east is from the west, so He also, for me, made it as though I had never been in those circumstances in the first place (Ps. 103:12).

As far as I or anyone else was concerned, my life was over, and oh, the instant peril and devastation that came over me at the realization that all hope was gone. But oh, what yearning God placed within my heart the very moment I was set free—the longing to share my hope in glory with as many lost, wounded souls as possible before time expires on us all! Be that as it may, it was there in the deep valley of testing that I gained the unshakable confidence to know that whenever the enemy comes in like a flood, the Spirit of the Lord our God will always be right there to lift a standard against him (Isa. 59:19). Sadly, it took nearly two more years for me to finally realize that God is for me, even though during that time He had completely rebuilt my broken life and vastly suppressed my disheartened past from causing further harm.

Charles Stanley, one of the most prolific Bible teachers of our time and someone who's had a taste of what it feels like to be alone and abandoned when he and his wife were divorced during the height of his ministry, said this: "When you become consumed by God's call on your life, everything will take on new meaning and significance. You will begin to see every facet of your life, including your pain, as a means through which God can work to bring others to Himself."

Without a doubt, I had a lot to learn about Christianity and myself regarding who I was as a Christian and what purpose God had for my life. Through it all, I found myself consumed with a strange fire burning in my heart to share this story of God's sovereign power and grace that brought hope, healing, love, life, and total restoration to my life with other lost, broken, and hurting souls! That's all I ever wanted to do!

However, that would prove to be an enormous challenge, considering how, for several years, I suffered from a severe case of what I would call "a spiritual identity crisis." Undoubtedly, I was set apart by God for a purpose, but what purpose? A career truck driver, someone involved in ministry, or both? If ministry, what type of ministry? I had served with Prison Fellowship briefly and loved working with inmates. I had been a church usher for a couple of years before moving to Smithville, Missouri, where I became a worship leader at a neighboring suburb of Kansas City at a little out-of-the-way-church, Calvary Chapel, located in Liberty, Missouri.

Later I found myself filling the pulpit while my pastor, Scott Gurwell, traveled back and forth to Southern California. And as exciting and rewarding as all that was, what I loved more than anything else was doing the work of an evangelist. I loved all those tremendous privileges, but something was still missing, and the check in my spirit said that none of it felt right! I believed that God had given me a strong burden to move to the mountains. The problem was that I'd always wanted to move to the mountains, and I couldn't imagine God sending me to a place I'd always wanted to be. No one had ever shown me that type of kindness! Yet, in any case, I knew if I ever did go, I would look for a place that needed a Bible-teaching church and start a fellowship.

But I still had the bug for travel and evangelism, and the more I tried to figure out my inner turmoil, the more frustrated I became. And even though I did enjoy serving as a worship leader, an usher, and my pastor's assistant—even filling the roll of a lead pastor after Peggi and I left Missouri—my heart was created for, gifted for, and prepared for evangelistic outreach, music, and restoration ministry. However, when Peggi and I did leave Missouri to move to South Dakota, it was for that purpose: to start a church with the hope of doing evangelistic outreaches as well. And while God did bless the work we started while in South Dakota, my heart was still unsure of who I was in Christ Jesus.

Jesus made a profound statement when He said, "Whoever finds his life will lose it, and whoever loses his life for My sake will find it" (Matt. 10:39)! He also said, "If you abide in My Word you are My disciples indeed. And you shall know the truth, and the truth shall make you free" (John 8:31–32). That was what I was searching for—the truth about who I am in Christ and the freedom to be who I am in Christ, along with His blessing and daily strength to walk in the works that were prepared beforehand for both Peggi and me to walk in (Eph. 2:10).

In the fall of 2010, following a three-day evangelistic outreach event that our organization hosted at Black Hills State University (in addition to our participation in school assemblies and evangelistic work with Rick and Mick Vigneulle), Peggi and I desperately needed to get away and spend some quiet time with God to seek His counsel and direction. We took a short drive down to Colorado to visit Ft. Collins and Colorado Springs. I'd always wanted to live in Colorado. I loved the dry climate and the smell of pine trees. But there is something about the mountains that always takes my breath away. What's more, we never had an actual honeymoon, so we were really looking forward to those few days away together.

If you read *The Potter and the Clay*, you probably remember the "Christian Love Story" chapter on how God brought Peggi's and my lives together while living in Missouri. But in case you haven't read it, I shared the story of how God told me the moment I first laid eyes on her that she was the girl I would marry and that she would follow me anywhere in the world that He wanted us to go. She was gorgeous and her personality was irresistibly feisty (in a very attractive and fun sense), but over and above, she was—and still is today—tenderhearted and sweet to the core. And after learning more about her, I began to wonder what a spectacular woman like that would need with a sojourner like me.

So one day, in a temporary moment of doubt and frustration, I asked God, "If this really is Your plan then, Lord, what exactly does a girl like that need with someone like me?" He said, "Nothing. You need her!" It didn't take long for that to make sense. And boy, do I need her—more and more and more each day! What she did need, though, and want more than anything was a strong spiritual leader who was not ashamed of the Gospel or the name of Jesus Christ, and who knew His calling. One who was comfortable in his own skin and would love, honor, and cherish every moment of their time together, and then finish the race set before them by God.

I know I've written quite a lot about Peggi in my last two books, but I'm still not sure it's enough. Proverbs 18:22 says, "He who finds a wife finds a good thing and obtains favor from the Lord!" God has given His favor and blessing on our marriage, and Peggi has never once hesitated to drop everything and go wherever God wanted us to go. As Peggi and I initially got to know each other, only then did I learn that she had traveled to countries in South America and India as a medical missionary. On one trip in particular, she had visited a remote and poverty-stricken village in India, breaking her heart to pieces and changing her life forever.

The more I got to know her, the more her love for Jesus Christ and her passion for broken people from all over the world became evident. And even after all these years of being married, I still find myself drifting off into the land of awe over both her and the grace of God that brought our lives together. I laugh at the silly things she does that make her so cute in her everyday life, like getting lost in a small town or going the wrong direction on the right road. I tell her jokingly that she could get lost going to the restroom at home without her GPS. But when it comes to knowing our Father's will and following the divine directions that God has given regarding crucial life decisions, she is my GPS!

She knew that South Dakota was not our permanent home, as far as this world was concerned, but neither of us knew how long we would be there or where that desired place was that we were searching for until that one beautiful, sunny Sunday morning at a little church in Ft. Collins, Colorado. That morning, God gave us clear and decisive directions through both His written Word and a word of prophecy that not only numbered our days in South Dakota but also opened the door to a remarkable hope and future for us in Colorado Springs.

At first, I thought that maybe God was directing us to the Ft. Collins area and possibly to that little church. Peggi wasn't so sure though and thought we needed to visit Colorado Springs before making any decisions. I agreed and was even eager to visit another small but thriving Calvary Chapel located on the north end of Colorado Springs that I knew shared my heart for evangelistic ministry, since I had visited their website some months earlier. A special neighborhood evangelistic outreach event had been posted on their site—an annual event hosted by their church, listing their vision for reaching their neighborhood and local community with the Gospel. The description of the event they had posted was a near carbon copy of the His Song Evangelistic events we had been doing for years in both Missouri and South Dakota. What's more, I couldn't wait to meet the front man for the band who was pictured on their website, Pastor George Arnold, the man leading the charge.

After reading his ministry bio, I told Peggi, "There is a man after my own heart." I learned that George had also served as both an assistant and a lead pastor for several years also, and how his passion for ministry was only satisfied when he was taking the Gospel to the dark and troubled back roads and valleys of society. He had been involved with prison ministries for over thirty years in both California and Colorado, and hoped to one day spend all his ministry time focused entirely on evangelistic outreach for inmates in Colorado prisons, many of whom would be returning to the vigorous challenges of society.

George and I became friends, and I had even been invited to speak at a couple of his prison services. I learned a lot about myself through my friendship with George, particularly how to embrace the person I was created to be in Christ Jesus. In many respects, my life mirrors that of the demoniac from Mark chapter five. Despite everything, God saw the true heart entrapped inside that tormented man, and He saw the potential locked away. God knew exactly who that person was and what he could one day become. Like Jesus, soon the entire world would know who this man was as a result of the personal encounter he had with Jesus Christ, Who, along with His disciples, crossed the Sea of Galilee against a great windstorm while in a boat that appeared to be in danger of sinking and endangering the lives of the crew. Nevertheless, Jesus and His disciples went to the other side, and the tormented man was delivered from Satan's grip, healed, and restored to his right mind (Mark 5:3–7).

I have said on occasion how I've seen my own story in Mark chapter five and how I represent a twenty-first century version of the demoniac. My story has not only been my greatest spiritual asset in ministering to lost, broken, and hurting people of my generation, but has also been the stone on which God used to build His Heart United Ministries in Christ Jesus. And although the name "demoniac" would be a badge of honor regarding persecutions, God said, "I have even called you by your name; I have named you, though you have not known Me. I am the Lord, and there is no other; there is no God besides Me. I will gird you, though you have not known Me, that they may know from the rising of the sun to its setting that there is none besides Me" (Isa. 45:4b–6a).

Finally, I will close this chapter with a short story about a legendary guitarist named Lester Estelle. As a child, Lester loved music and somehow managed to teach himself how to play the guitar, holding it upside down and backward. He would watch guitarists on TV and began to mirror their image. In the process, Lester created his own unique style and method for playing guitar and became extremely talented at it; in fact, he became one of the elite guitar players of all time.

Over the years, however, people questioned his unique gift, insisting that if he were to be taken serious as a musician, he would have to stop playing pretend and learn how to play the guitar the correct way. And although that had never stopped him from creating music and melodies, he started to believe his critics and spent nearly three years learning the traditional approach to playing guitar.

Lester shared that story at a His Heart United event here in Colorado, explaining how frustrating it was to try to please his critics by fitting into a mold that just didn't fit, nor was he created for. It wasn't until God spoke to Lester about his unique gifting and how he himself was unique and created for that purpose that his attitude began to change. God pointed out that he was created to play his unique style of musicianship for His glory as a one-of-a-kind testimony to the world.

Lester's gift has inspired people of all levels of society around the world. He was designed for that very purpose: to encourage others to strive with all their heart, soul, mind, and strength to find their own unique purpose and spiritual gifting, and to not waste a single second of their lives trying to be anything other than what they were created by their Father in heaven to be!

My dad used to say, "Son, you can't see the forest for the trees." I never really understood a lot of his fatherly terminology or wisdom back then, but it makes perfect sense to me now. It took fourteen years in the wilderness on a long journey through three different states before I finally learned that God had already been working out His plan for my life all that time right before my very eyes. I had somehow become oblivious to the work God had already been doing in and through and around my life all those years. I am what I am by the revelation and grace of my Almighty God and Savior, Jesus Christ, and that's good enough for me!

I don't call myself a pastor, nor do I call myself an evangelist. I am a sinner saved by grace on a mission to be the very best witness I can be for the glory of God in Christ Jesus and for the hope and great future that God has prepared in advance for the countless broken souls that have no idea they are wanted by God, and for the few severely shattered ones who are so precious in the eyes of God that they are not just wanted—they are God's Most Wanted!

Today, my focus is telling the world what great things God has done in my life and what great mercy He has bestowed on my once-shattered existence. In addition, I seek to share how God redeemed the irredeemable and made all things new again just as He promised He would do! "What is man, that You are mindful of him, or the son of man, that You care for him? You made him for a little while lower than the angels; yet You have crowned him with glory and honor" (Heb. 2:6–7)! Thank You, Lord Jesus! Amen!

CHAPTER 11

THE PRICE IS RIGHT

As a child, I loved watching the television game show *The Price is Right*. Whoever envisioned the concept was brilliantly in tune to the foolish nature of the human heart—especially when it comes to the nail-biting suspense of watching critical decisions being made by people encountering high-pressure temptation. The finalist would be given the opportunity to keep what material treasure they had accumulated and secured through their winnings or spin the wheel in hope of an even greater treasure hidden behind one of any number of curtains.

The catch is that the wrong choice could cost you everything. On the other hand, the right choice, the right curtain, could mean treasure beyond imagination! In any case, life and the true riches of this life, in many ways, are like *The Price is Right*, only backward. In real life, there's no such thing as luck or chance; there's only faith and the choice between two destinies: one with Jesus Christ and one without Him. The ultimate reality for both destinies is hidden behind the veil of eternity. In a similar way, the wrong choices in this life can cost you everything, including family, love, homes, happiness, and the most costly—eternal life with Christ.

Every day we encounter new choices, a new set of curtains, new temptations, and new opportunities. The difference in real life is that we may either walk by faith or walk by sight. Faith means staking your claim on the wisdom of another, while sight means holding on to what we have and relying on our own wisdom and understanding. In life, the stakes are much higher!

God has provided me with faithful friendships and priceless counsel from a handful of His great men of tremendous faith and unshakable character, namely Justin Alfred, Jim Manning, and David Lin. All three are still anchors for my life that serve to mentor me and steady me through the rough perils of life's greatest tempest and spiritual storms. However, they only serve to offer me clear and decisive direction based on their vast knowledge of Christian service and living accumulated through the years of manning their own vessels through life's fierce and turbulent passing winds of destructive doctrines and toils.

Nonetheless, even with the finest counsel that heaven offers, I am still the captain at the helm of my own vessel, and the controls were left to my discretion. I make those critical decisions and bear the responsibilities and consequences for those choices. And I must confess, I've had serious doubts and restless nights at different seasons of my spiritual journey, especially when these three trusted brothers and faithful mentors would instruct me to shore up my sails, steer straight into the storm, and stay the course! Each time, though, the Lord would guide this beaten and battered vessel made of dirt and clay safely through those troubled waters to the other side. Moreover, something spectacular and completely unexpected would always accrue at the end of each of those potentially destructive trials that would remind me of the divine providence and unmatchable power of Christ. He would leave me humbled, awakened, and, at times, broken all over again! But the roughest and most tempting stretch of the journey that taught me the most about my true self started on September 1, 2001, and finally ended on April 19, 2004.

I begged God to calm the storm. I felt like He had abandoned me to the will and pleasure of my adversary. Today, however, I can honestly testify that there was purpose in the storm and that this was nothing out of the ordinary when sailing across life's seas with Jesus Christ. If it's the true and imperishable treasures that we desire, such as love, commitment, security, etc., then trials, opposition, and suffering should not only be expected but also embraced.

Jesus, as recorded in Mark chapter four, said to His disciples, "Let us go over to the other side." So, leaving the crowd behind, they took Him along, just as He was, in the boat. There were also other boats with Him. So, what is the value in telling us two thousand years after the fact that there were other boats with them? It is priceless—especially with this book being written with the many broken and storm-tossed people in mind who are feeling battered, abandoned, and alone. Jesus wants us to fully understand that no matter how severe the storm, we're never alone for He is always with us in the storm. He will never leave us or forsake us, no matter how bad the situation may get. There is comfort in knowing that we are not the only one going through life's storms!

Peter, who was in that boat, said, "Be of sober spirit, be on the alert. Your adversary, the devil, prowls around like a roaring lion, seeking someone to devour. But resist him, firm in your faith, knowing that the same experiences of suffering are being accomplished by your brethren who are in the world. After you have suffered for a little while, the God of all grace, Who called you to His eternal glory in Christ, will Himself perfect, confirm, strengthen and establish you" (1 Pet. 5:8–11).

But the story tells of a furious windstorm that suddenly arose, and the waves began to break over the boat so that it was nearly full and, according to the disciples (who, by the way, were seasoned sailors who made their living as fishermen in troubled waters), appeared to be sinking beneath the crashing waves of hopelessness. Jesus, however, was in the stern of the vessel sleeping on a cushion, impervious through the storm. The disciples woke Him and said to Him, "Teacher, don't You care if we perish?" He arose, rebuked the wind, and said to the waves, "Peace! Be still!" Then the wind died down and was completely calm. He said to His disciples, "Why are you so afraid? Oh, you of little faith?" They were terrified and asked each other, "Who is this? Even the wind and the waves obey Him" (Mark 4:35–41)!

In John chapter sixteen, Jesus was forewarning His disciples of an even bigger storm on the horizon, and that not only would the world forsake Him, but He would also be betrayed by one of His closest confidants, put to death, and His disciples would abandon Him also. But even then, when the whole world including His closest and seemingly more trusted inner circle of friends forsook Him, He declared that even then He would still not be alone, for His Father would be with Him.

The truth is, we may encounter times when it seems like we have been left alone at life's gallows. Even in my darkest hour following the events of March 6, 1997, after all the damage I had done, the Father was right there with me in the storm which I was certain had ended my life. I was convinced that my situation was hopeless, as God had every logical and practical reason to give up, write me off, and move on as most of society already had. But He saw beyond those momentary circumstances—things that were simply impossible for me to see through that horrific storm. God knew the plans He had for my life and saw a life so far beyond my belief as a result of how He would use all that evil and suffering for good!

Without the events of March 6, 1997, I wouldn't be who I am today. Nor would I be about my Father's business every day when I step out of the house and enter life's courtroom, testifying before a world of human judges of the enormity of Christ Jesus, the uncontestable hope of the world! Jesus will always be with us, passing through the waters of temptation and doubt and through every fiery affliction we will ever encounter. For the believer, these circumstances will be used to strengthen our faith; for the unbeliever, they will provide faith! The question was and still is today asked by Jesus: "Do you believe?"

"'Indeed the hour is coming,' said our Lord, 'yes, has now come, that you will be scattered, [speaking to His closest followers who were there with Him just prior to Him be crucified; but unfortunately, this very thing is occurring all over again in America and around the world today].'" He said that each would go to own, and they would leave Him alone. Yet He said, "I am not alone, because the Father is with Me. These things I have spoken to you, that in Me you may have peace. In the world you will have tribulation; but be of good cheer, I have overcome the world" (John 16:31–33)!

International critically acclaimed bestselling author Haruki Murakami said this about life's storms: "Once the storm is over, you won't remember how you made it through or how you managed to survive. You won't even be sure, whether the storm is really over. But one thing is certain. When you come out of the storm, you won't be the same person who went in. That's what this storm's all about."

For me, the only place where I truly began to know Jesus Christ intimately and have the confidence to be able to rest in His saving and sustaining grace was when I discovered the courage to trust Jesus completely. When life left me no other choice but to let go of the world I was holding onto, die in my unbelief, or accept Jesus's invitation to trust Him, I chose Him! And even as this earthen vessel appeared to be capsizing, ready to plunge deep beneath the crashing waves of life's troubled waters to the bedrock bottom of hopelessness, that's where I experienced the power of Jesus Christ's redeeming love! Without the living God right there in this storm-tossed, battered vessel anchoring me to Himself, I would have perished.

I understand how so many wonderful people are suffering as a result of someone else's decisions and that life is simply not fair. But again, this is a trustworthy statement written to help us put our suffering to rest and close the door to the past for good. I can promise you with absolute certainty that there is joy in a life fully committed to Christ—so great that it can erase any unmerited pain you may have encountered and remove painful scars that you thought could never be removed once and for all!

Paul, quoting King Solomon (who, like me, also experienced this promise become a reality in his life), said, "'Eye has not seen, nor ear heard, nor have entered into the heart of man the things which God has prepared for those who love Him.' But God has revealed them to us through His Spirit. For the Spirit searches all things, yes, the deep things of God. For what man knows the things of a man except the spirit of the man which is in him? Even so no one knows the things of God except the Spirit of God. Now we have received, not the spirit of the world, but the Spirit Who is from God, that we might know the things that have been freely given to us by God" (1 Cor. 2:9–12)!

The truth is we were all God's workmanship created in Christ Jesus to fulfill an abundant life beyond all we could think or imagine, ordained by God Himself before time began (Eph. 2:10–3:20). But not only are we the only ones who can live that life, but life itself will be hidden in Christ Jesus up to that moment of truth when we finally surrender our lives completely to Him and His Spirit dwells richly in our hearts in all wisdom, teaching, and admonishing (Col. 3:16). Otherwise, we will never know what true life and living is like.

In other words, as David said, until Jesus Christ is the center and object of our daily devotion and we are filled with His Spirit, the desires of our hearts will continue to elude us (Ps. 37:4). Why? Because no one can know the true riches of God apart from the Spirit of God. The person without the Spirit does not accept the things that come from the Spirit of God but consider them foolishness. It's foolishness because they cannot understand them; they are discerned only through the Spirit of God (1 Cor. 2:14).

When the Lord instructed me after becoming a Christian to love my enemies and bless those who curse me, I thought it sounded ludicrous! And if a genuine born-again believer who desperately wants to know and please his Kinsman Redeemer thinks it sounds foolish, you can only imagine what a nonbeliever would think! Jesus asked, "If you love those who love you, what reward have you? Do not even the tax collectors do the same? And if you greet your brethren only, what do you do more than others?" (Matt. 5:46–47).

We are to keep our behavior excellent among the Gentiles so that in the thing in which they slander us as evildoers, they may—though, no guarantees—because of our charitable deeds (as they observe them over an extended period of time), glorify God in the day of their own visitation (1 Pet. 2:12). We can only accomplish this by fixing our eyes on Jesus, the Author and Perfecter of faith, Who for the joy set before Him endured the cross, despising the shame, and has sat down at the right hand of the throne of God (Heb. 12:2)!

That is what the writer of Hebrews meant when he said, "Without faith it is impossible to please God," because anyone who comes to Him must believe that He exists and that He rewards those who earnestly seek Him (Heb. 11:6)! However, if you are bitterly jealous and keep selfish ambition in your heart, you are instructed to not cover up the truth with boasting and lying. In other words, don't let your emotions sink your boat! Cease from anger and forsake wrath; it only causes harm (Ps. 37:8). Or, as Paul said, "Be angry, and do not sin: do not let the sun go down on your wrath" (Eph. 4:26).

The wrath of man does not produce the righteousness of God (James 1:20), but it will most certainly bring down the wrath of God on those who think vengeance is theirs. Paul forewarned us as believers about misrepresenting God before a world of nonbelievers, asking this rhetorical question: "Do you show contempt for the riches of His kindness, forbearance and patience, not realizing that God's kindness is intended to lead you to repentance?" (Rom. 2:4). We are to beware of our own stubbornness and unrepentant hearts, realizing that we could be storing up wrath against ourselves for the day of God's wrath, when His righteous judgment will be revealed (Rom. 2:5).

Jealousy and selfishness are not God's kind of wisdom but rather are earthly, unspiritual, and demonic (James 3:14–15)! Wow, could this have been the cancer that destroyed the demoniac's life? I don't know, but after the disciples in Mark chapter four weathered the storm (which had been allowed for their own benefit), they finally reached the other side, and it was there where they witnessed the demoniac being rescued and delivered at the hands of the same Jesus Who had just calmed the raging storm earlier that evening. Jesus then sent the man away, telling him to go home to his family and friends and share what great things God had done for him and what great mercy God had bestowed on his formerly shattered life. In response, the man went to the northern region of Decapolis, preaching the good news of Jesus Christ. He became a mighty evangelist and quite possibly could have been the voice echoing across the region that caused the four thousand men (not counting women and children) to gather for what is known as the feeding of the four thousand, listed just three chapters later in Mark chapter eight!

Likewise, it was on April 19, 2004, when I witnessed a similar deliverance taking place at the home of my dear friend and close brother in Christ, Mark Webb! I look back and think about that remarkable encounter between Mark and the Lord and the blistering, opposing winds that arose and lasted for three long years prior to his deliverance at the hand of the same Jesus Who, two thousand years earlier, calmed the troubled sea and rescued and restored the demoniac—and Who later did the same for me on March 6,1997.

Had it not been for the work He did in my heart in the midst of that troublesome season of my life, there probably wouldn't be any point in my writing this book. I would not have had anything to offer. Nevertheless, at that time, I thought the Lord must have fallen asleep during Satan's attempt to drown me in the sea of life's unforgiving waters! But now I don't know how much credit Satan really deserves when in all three cases our Lord was disciplining His followers—first in the case of His disciples crossing the Sea of Galilee, then in the cases of Mark Webb (a nonbeliever at the time) and me (a young Christian learning valuable life lessons) as we were passing through our own version of life's troubled waters.

When I read about the faith of the early Christians, their costly struggles, and the fierce opposition they encountered, it puts things into perspective once more. I'm so grateful to have a Father Who loves me so much that He would spend three years correcting and training this son for a future purpose of working in the family business, especially when the family business involves reigning and ruling forever alongside the One Who endured the worst suffering of all times for me. The writer of Hebrews reminded us of that very thing, saying, "In our struggle against sin, we have not yet resisted to the point of shedding our blood [as Christ had done]." Furthermore, the author asked if we had completely forgotten this word of encouragement that addresses us as a father addresses his children: "My son, do not make light of the Lord's discipline, and do not lose heart when He rebukes you, because the Lord disciplines the one He loves, and He chastens everyone He accepts as His son."

Endure hardship as discipline, for this is God's way of treating us as His children. For what children are not disciplined by their father? If you are not disciplined—and everyone undergoes discipline—then you are not legitimate, not true sons and daughters at all (Heb. 12:4–8)! Jesus taught us that the curtain—the one that has been so despised and has for this present age been temporarily veiled—is, in fact, the right door that leads to joy everlasting. And the best news is we don't have to wait till we die to receive it. We are given the Holy Spirit Who leads us into all truth.

Jesus also said, "I am the door. If anyone enters by Me, he will be saved, and will go in and out and find pasture." Good pasture is the life-changing, life-giving power of the Word of God. At the same time, the question remains: which curtain/door will you choose? Which life do you desire? Over and above, where do you want to spend eternity?

The true riches offered to us in this rapidly passing life are not comprised of material things that are here one moment and gone the next. The Scripture calls these "uncertain riches" and warns us not to trust in them (1 Tim. 6:17). The true riches are "To know the love of Christ, which passeth knowledge" and to be "filled with all the fullness of God" (Eph. 3:19). So, in everything, if we behave toward others the same way we would have them do toward us, then that sums up the whole Law and the Prophets (Matt. 7:12)! We are to be careful how we walk, not as unwise men but as wise, redeeming the time, knowing that the days are evil (Eph. 5:15).

Although being filled with the wisdom from above is a great blessing which gives us a tremendous advantage regarding critical life decisions, it doesn't necessarily guarantee a trouble-free life. King Solomon was known far and wide for his wisdom; nonetheless, he didn't always heed the counsel of his own conscience. He made numerous decisions that resulted in catastrophic consequences, causing him to sum life up as vanity, all is vanity! Likewise, the greatest lessons I've learned since becoming a follower of Jesus Christ is mostly how desperately wicked and deceitful my heart still is, and how now, more than any time before, I need the favor, wisdom, and guidance of Jesus Christ in my daily walk with Him.

Before I became a Christian, I only had my own reputation to think about, and frankly, I didn't care what people thought of me. However, it's no longer about my reputation but the integrity of God's character and the preservation of the Gospel that I care about. I most certainly don't want to be responsible for anyone missing the opportunity of salvation and heaven based on my actions and how they, as unbelievers, perceive God's heart of love and compassion toward them as a result of those actions. I can't think of anything more selfish, arrogant, or dangerous than letting my emotions run amuck and being the reason for someone missing their place in eternity with God.

Paul's instructions for the church were elementary, admonishing us to conduct ourselves with wisdom toward outsiders, making the most of the opportunity. He said to let our speech always be with grace, as though seasoned with salt, so that we will know how we should respond to each person (Col. 4:5–6). God Himself will require our witness to be much more than just an outward appearance. Furthermore, our witness will be nothing more than a hypocritical expression of our own heart until it becomes a genuine reflection of the heart of Jesus Christ—a heart filled with a love so true that it kept Him nailed to the cross for six agonizing hours, regarding our futures, our happiness, and our well-being to be more important than His own life!

Jesus said, "Greater love hath no man than this, that a man lay down his life for his friends" (John 15:13)! So, if it's purpose, healing, love, and life that you desire, then undoubtedly you crave a desirable thing that certainly lines up with the will of God. The only thing that could prevent you from finding your hidden treasure is you! If you heed the counsel of our Mighty Lord and Savior Jesus Christ, you can't go wrong. He said, "Love your enemies, bless those who curse you, do good to those who hate you, and pray for those who spitefully use you and persecute you, that you may be sons of your Father in heaven; for He makes His sun rise on the evil and on the good, and sends rain on the just and on the unjust" (Matt. 5:44–45)! Isn't that exactly what Jesus Christ did for you and me?

I will conclude this chapter with the following quote from Thomas R. Steagald:

> You shall love the Lord your God with all
> your heart, and with all your soul, and with all
> your mind. This is the first and greatest com-

mandment. And the second is like it, you shall love your neighbor as yourself. The first command was clear and absolute, unalterable and unchanging. But there was a loophole in the second—wiggle room if we do not love ourselves. So at dinner Jesus tightened the loop, closed the hole: "A new command I give you, that you love one another as I have loved you." (Thomas R. Steagald, *Every Disciple's Journey: Following Jesus to a God-Focused Faith*)

Amen!

CHAPTER 12

IRON SHARPENS IRON II
PART I: FAITH, HOPE, AND LOVE

The great relationship that I both covet and enjoy so much today with my great friend and brother in Christ, Mark Webb, represents a classic God moment that began as two determined hearts indignantly at war against each other—believer versus nonbeliever—engaged in a heated three-year conflict that ultimately exposed the indifference of both hearts, leaving us both broken before God with far more questions than we had answers for.

The root cause of the conflict was centered around Jesus Christ, His crucifixion, and the authenticity of the Holy Bible! Fortunately, though, and unlike most differences, this was a conflict with a divine purpose that would enhance the understanding of both hearts. Even in the storm, God was doing far more than simply working all things together for my good—He was also about to level the playing field for both Mark and me that would make both the winner.

Today, I share this story to testify how this war had a remarkable ending, resulting in Mark Webb being saved and my heart being humbled through the disciplinary teaching of our Lord. Our differences were used to help sharpen our character in the same way that "As iron sharpens iron, so one man sharpens another" (Prov. 27:17). Just as iron sharpens iron and brings out the good in many of God's chosen vessels, it also exposes the worst of wickedness existing within many hearts that, as Christians, we may not have even been aware was there. But without hesitation, I must confess—I couldn't have been more wrong!

This turned out to be a classic demonstration of the unsearchable wisdom of God molding two hearts like clay in the Potter's hands. I honestly believe it was those three years that not only defined who I am as a believer, but also saved my future by restoring a very deep-rooted Christ-centered love and compassion that had been missing since my childhood! Mark, however, couldn't understand for the longest time how a kind and loving God could allow so much trouble and violence in this suffering world. He disliked and resented nearly all professing Christians, insisting that not only did God not exist, but also that the Bible was nothing more than a weak man's crutch for cowardly people who couldn't handle life. I was simply appalled and found nothing whatsoever amusing about Mark's adolescent behavior toward Jesus or the Bible. In fact, the fool has said in his heart, "There is no God." They are corrupt; they have done abominable works; there is none who does good.

I was a very unapologetically outspoken follower of Jesus Christ after the encounter that healed and restored my former broken life. But still, I had a lot to learn about the kindness of the Lord. That same passage also says, "The Lord looks down from heaven upon the children of men, to see if there are any who understand, who seek God." Sadly, it took those three difficult years for me to accept the truth that "They have all turned aside, they have together become corrupt; there is none who does good, no, not one" (Ps. 14:2–3).

I had done my absolute best to live a life pleasing to my Lord, and with all my heart I sincerely wanted to be a great witness for Him. But nonetheless, the verdict was in, and the evidence was indisputable—my heart was not as wicked as Mark's, who was an unbeliever; it was far worse than Mark's. The Apostle Paul said that we can have all the gifts in the universe, but without love, our faith is nothing. "If I speak in the tongues of men or of angels, but do not have love, I am only a resounding gong or a clanging cymbal. If I have the gift of prophecy and know all mysteries and have all knowledge, and if I have a faith that can move mountains, but do not have love, I am nothing" (1 Cor. 13:1–4)!

I had missed the mark by a mile, and though that might be expected from a nonbeliever, I was very disappointed to learn how far I had drifted from where I began just seven years earlier, further away from the goal of what I hoped to become. But amazingly, instead of punishment, Mark and I were both covered in God's mercy and united together by His grace! We were now standing together on a level playing field, brothers in Christ, overwhelmed with love and gratitude that our stains had been removed. Additionally, we were overcome by the immeasurable riches of God's foreknowledge and longsuffering toward two undeserving souls that He had, for whatever reasons, chosen to represent Him before this dark and troubled world. But none of that would come before He strategically used those three years to teach us how to love others as Christ first loved us.

> Love is patient, love is kind. It does not envy, it does not boast, it is not proud. It does not dishonor others, it is not self-seeking, it is not easily angered, it keeps no record of wrongs. Love does not delight in evil but rejoices with the truth. It always protects, always trusts, always hopes, always perseveres. Love never fails. (1 Cor. 13:5–8)!

I was in the early stages of preparing for a life that God had prepared for me—including my wonderful marriage to my beloved wife, Peggi Sue—but before God could do that, He would have to begin by doing a work in my heart to perfect that which concerns me! It all came to a head on April 19, 2004, when God instructed me to set aside all my personal feelings and go share the Gospel with Mark at his home in Kansas City. God wanted Mark to know how much He loves him and how Jesus Christ died on a cross for both his sins and mine, and that the only real difference between he and I was the salvation that sets us apart in Jesus Christ, my hope in glory (Col. 1:27).

In like manner, Mark needed to know that God, Who knows the end from the beginning, along with every sin, sorrow, pain, suffering, and failure encountered over the course of his life, that he was God's chosen. He too was wanted by God. And just as our Father had a plan prepared for my life, He also had a plan for his life.

Later that night after I left Mark's home, Mark's life forever changed when he was shown a vision of heaven. He immediately surrendered his life to Jesus and to the will of our gracious Father. Two hearts once divided were now united together on a mission. We became inseparable on our quest to bring God's message of hope through Christ Jesus to other broken lives. Like the demoniac, Mark also became a powerful evangelist. His heart was so broken over the arrogant man he had been before God revealed to him the truth that changed his life, and he wanted the world to know that truth!

Like Paul though, Mark had despised Christians before he encountered Jesus Christ. The reason this story is so relevant to this book, like the "Iron Sharpens Iron" story shared in *The Potter and the Clay*, is because it further demonstrates the reality of life's priceless hidden treasures that are buried deep beneath the many layers of bitterness, resentments, jealously, stubborn pride, and self-centeredness that turns the hearts of both believers and nonbelievers alike hard as stone. In like manner, Hosea, fed up with the wickedness of those of his generation, said, "Sow for yourselves righteousness; reap in mercy; break up your fallow ground, for it is time to seek the Lord, till He comes and rains righteousness on you" (Hos. 10:12)!

A.W. Tozar paints a beautiful word portrait of Hosea's analogy regarding human hearts and fallow ground. Tozar writes, "The one whose heart is hard or followed has fenced himself in, and by the same act he has fenced out God and the miracle." Like a fallow field, says Tozar, "It is paying a terrible price for its tranquility: never does it see the miracle of growth; never does it feel the motions of mounting life nor see the wonders of bursting seed nor the beauty of ripening grain. Fruit it can never know because it is afraid of the plow and the harrow...The plowed life is the life that has, in the act of repentance, thrown down the protecting fences and sent the plow of confession into the soul. The urge of the Spirit, the pressure of circumstances and the distress of fruitless living have combined thoroughly to humble the heart. Such a life has put away defense, and has forsaken the safety of death for the peril of life. Discontent, yearning, contrition, courageous obedience to the will of God: these have bruised and broken the soil till it is ready again for the seed. And as always, fruit follows the plow. Life and growth begin as God 'rains down righteousness.' Such a one can testify, 'And the hand of the Lord was upon me there' (Ezek. 3:22)."

How God used the common dislike Mark and I once had for each other amazingly demonstrates the truth regarding the mysterious reality that eye has not seen, nor ear heard, nor has it entered into the heart of man such amazing things which God has prepared for those who love Him (1 Cor. 2:9)! How could God take a borderline explosive coexistence and turn it into a weapon of warfare for good, annihilating hatred in the process with a love so strong and contagious that it could only be fit for heaven? I don't know! But this much I do know: that amazing season of testing capped off by that unprecedented God moment had just entered the preliminary stages of becoming a priceless portion of my life that I wouldn't have missed for all the money in the world. However, apart from my life in Christ, this beautiful treasure in disguise would have passed me by like a ship in the night along with the healing hand of God that turned the deep sorrows of my broken past into a volcanic eruption of joy unthinkable with purpose far beyond the limits of what my natural mind could ever conceive!

"When I was a child," said the Apostle Paul, "I used to speak like a child, think like a child, and reason like a child; when I became a man, I did away with childish things. For now we see in a mirror dimly, but then face to face; now I know in part, but then I will know fully just as I also have been fully known. But now faith, hope, love, abide these three; but the greatest of these is love" (1 Cor. 13:11–123)! And finally, Peter said, "Above all, love each other deeply, because love covers over a multitude of sins" (1 Pet. 4:8)!

CHAPTER 13

Iron Sharpens Iron II
Part II: The Morning After

News about Mark's salvation spread quickly, and just two months after he committed his life to Christ, he was asked to share his story at a church in Branson, Missouri, where his older brother was senior pastor. Many hearts were touched, and not long after that, he shared his testimony again with our congregation in Liberty, Missouri.

My heart was so moved that I asked him to share it again at what has since become a benchmark event that was planned for my hometown in Stanberry, Missouri—the event that I credit to opening my eyes to my own future by igniting the fire for evangelism that blazed across three states before finally landing in Colorado Springs, where it has now become His Heart United, a Network of Christian Ministries united together by God to reach the lost and restore other broken lives.

Mark poured his heart out with amazing passion, touching many lives as he began to share his journey from brokenness to heaven's gate. Mark wasn't bashful about sharing how God had intervened in his life—transforming a former egocentric narcissist into a product of God's grace and now unashamed follower of Christ—and what Jesus Christ means to him now! It was soon obvious that Mark had the heart of an evangelist with a rare gift to communicate Christ's passion for the lost and broken to complete strangers practically everywhere he went, including grocery stores, businesses, his local neighborhood, work, and beyond. People would often say to him, "There is something different about you." That would open the door for Mark to share his faith in Jesus and what it was that made him different.

Undoubtedly, there is something different about people filled with the light of Jesus. I believe the peace and light of the Lord can be seen by most people and is irresistibly attractive. It especially stands out when in the company of nonbelievers. Our witness is a visible manifestation of the light of Jesus Christ that He alone distributes and a light that can only be seen in the life of someone who has been with the Lord and in whom the Spirit of the Lord dwells.

One example of this is found in Exodus 34:35 when Moses petitioned God to show him His glory and later when he addressed the sons of Israel. During those times, the people visually saw the glory of God on his face. A similar thing happened in the New Testament book of Acts, which says, "The members of the council were amazed when they saw the boldness of Peter and John, for they could see that they were ordinary men with no special training in the Scriptures. They also recognized them as men who had been with Jesus" (Acts 4:13).

In *The Potter and the Clay*, I wrote about the morning after April 19, 2004—the first time anyone had seen Mark as a born-again Christian. I was at work in a room full of other Estes drivers, waiting on my delivery papers before starting my work day. From my vantage point, I had a clear view of the parking lot when Mark showed up for work. Most of the guys in that room were not followers of Jesus Christ, but nonetheless, each one noticed something different about Mark's puzzling countenance. Obviously, something had changed; this was not the same Mark Webb.

In trying to find the right words to explain my reaction, it was as though the Holy Spirit could hardly contain His joy as He bore witness to me confirming that this was not just a passing fad; rather, something had transpired between Him and Mark shortly after I'd left Mark's house the night before, and Mark would never be the same. I recognized the light in him from across the parking lot.

I also described in *The Potter and the Clay* how a handful of precious souls where I grew up at Stanberry, Missouri, stood out from the rest of society during my time there. They were so different, kind, loving, and beautiful in every way. The light of our Redeemer would radiate in and out from them, so bright that I simply could not comprehend that light. I mentioned the impression made on my heart by my late mother, Mary Jeanette Lucas, her wonderful best friend and a precious soul, Jean Adams, and others. I mentioned my childhood pastor and now wonderful friend, Pastor Dick Lionburger, as well as a tremendous man of God and a Christ-centered reflection of the Lord Himself, Bill Noble.

Bill was a friend of our family, an appliance tech and local business owner who, out of the kindness of his heart and a radical love for Jesus Christ, spent much of his time fixing people's broken appliances as a means of sharing the love of Jesus with our community, giving no regard whatsoever to money. Bill would always, in a masterful and loving way, remind me of how Jesus loved me, gave His life on a cross for me, and died to remove my sins and stains for good!

I also shared how the memories of those remarkable God-fearing saints flooded my mind the day my former life ended in that Clay County Missouri Jail on March 6, 1997. Undoubtedly, they would be listed among the illuminating lights Jesus referred to when He said, "You are the light of the world—a city on a hilltop that cannot be hidden" (Matt. 5:14), the meek but mighty men and women of God, of whom the world is not worthy (Heb. 11:38)!

Mark was beaming with that glowing and transparent light when I saw him the morning after Jesus Christ touched his heart and ignited his spirit and mind with fire, love, compassion, and life. The change transformed Mark's personality and disposition so much that even members of his own family didn't recognize the new Mark Webb. He looked like Mark, but his demeanor had drastically changed.

Jesus warned us how the world could not comprehend His magnificent light. John records, "In Him was life, and the life was the light of men. And the light shines in the darkness, and the darkness does not comprehend it" (John 1:3–4). When Mark told his family that he had met Jesus Christ and was now a Bible-believing, born-again Christian, some were convinced that he may have had a mental breakdown and need to be committed to a hospital where he could be examined and diagnosed, get medications, counseling, psychiatric care, or whatever else the doctor might prescribe to treat Mark's illness that was causing his strange behavior, hoping to bring him back into his right mind. But the old Mark was gone, and the new Mark was finally in his right mind. He had been crucified with Christ, and it was no longer he who lived but Christ living in him (Gal. 2:20).

The Greatest Physician of the universe had already diagnosed Mark long ago. He was a sinner destined for hell, had God not already provided the cure for his condition on a wretched wooden cross at Mount Calvary. Remember what took place after Jesus healed the demoniac? "They came to Jesus and saw the demon-possessed man, the one who had had the legion, sitting there, clothed and in his right mind, and they were afraid" (Mark 5:15).

Mark was healed. What's more, Mark was made alive for the first time since he was born of flesh and blood! He was now born again of the Spirit of the living God! What caused so much confusion for others was confirmation for me. Mark wasn't well-received as a Christian by his immediate family or well-liked in other certain circles. But that came as no shock to me, because all those things had already happened to me years before. Furthermore, Jesus Himself was not well-received or liked. Jesus warned us that following Him would not be easy, saying, "If the world hates you, remember that the world hated Me first" (John 15:18)!

This gives credence to why the Lord is close to those with a broken heart and a contrite spirit (Ps. 34:18). He too experienced the pain of rejection, hatred, and abandonment. We do not have a high priest who is unable to sympathize with our weaknesses, but one Who, in every respect, has been tempted as we are, yet without sin (Heb. 4:15). "Contrite" in Hebrew means "crushed in spirit." No one knows that better than Jesus. Therefore, when coming to Christ, we come to Him as to a living stone rejected by men, yet choice and precious in the sight of God.

Remember the words that were heard around the world: "This is my beloved Son, with Whom I am well pleased" (Matt. 3:17)! God has these exact thoughts toward all who are broken and bruised and, like Moses, chose to be mistreated along with the people of God rather than to enjoy the fleeting pleasures of sin (Heb. 11:25).

Mark resisted God right up to the end, not knowing that he was created for God's purpose. Nor did he know he had been endowed with a unique ability to light the candles of so many other lost and hurting souls in dark and troubled places, illuminating the paths before so many that lead to that narrow gate which opens unto salvation. He began reaching so many dock workers and drivers at work that it became next to impossible to keep up with.

Then one day he asked me to help him start an after-hours Bible study at work for our coworkers. A couple of weeks later, a great spiritual revival began breaking out on a scale that I had never seen before or experienced. And not only were people coming to faith in Christ in record numbers, but our terminal also had mysteriously become the number-one ranked terminal in the Estes system nationwide. God was powerfully at work in that place.

We visited our boss's church for a special baptism night to support our coworkers who had come to Christ and were now being baptized for the first time. It was an emotional night, and I've never seen another like it. And while it was undoubtedly a remarkable season where both believers and nonbelievers alike witnessed a powerful manifestation of the Holy Spirit at work, it was short-lived and counterpunched by the furious Satan and soon came to a bittersweet end within weeks at the Estes Express Lines in Kansas City, Kansas.

Sadly, a handful of Estes employees, led by one man in particular—an angry driver named George—were taking turns calling the home office to complain about us doing a Bible study at work. We went to great lengths to make sure it was done behind closed doors and after work hours out of respect for others, but in any case, Satan was determined to quench that fire at all cost.

One afternoon while returning from my St. Joseph, Missouri route, I received a call from a friend who worked in the front office, warning me that a couple of corporate bosses from Chicago and Dallas had made a special trip to Kansas City to talk to Mark and me about the Bible study taking place on company grounds. I called Mark to ask if he knew. He did not know but was ecstatic to hear the news. He considered it a tremendous honor to possibly lose our jobs for being associated with the name of Jesus Christ. I remember thinking, *really?* At any rate, nothing was going to penetrate the impenetrable shield of faith guaranteed to cover and protect our peace, joy, and courage through any situation in this life.

The two men met with us in private, and to my surprise, the gentleman, whom we both knew from the Dallas terminal, looked at me and said, "I don't know what to do with you guys under these circumstances. I have never been asked to tell people not to practice their faith, and I certainly don't want to get on God's bad side." In a very classy manner, he politely asked if we would work with him and voluntarily move the Bible study off campus. We agreed and thanked him for being so considerate toward us after being sent hundreds of miles on our behalf when there were so many other things that needed his attention.

Not long after that, George, the gentleman who was leading the charge against us, was diagnosed with stage four lung cancer and was told he had only a short time to live. That's where I witnessed Jesus starting to shine through the life of my precious brother Mark Webb! Mark reached out to George by phone to let him know we were all thinking of him and asked if there was anything we could do for him. George, in tears, asked Mark if he would pray for him and his family. Mark soon led George to the Lord and never missed an opportunity to stop by to visit George and read Scriptures to him from the Bible.

God, working through Mark, prepared George's heart for his journey to heaven. And on the final leg of his earthly life, George asked Mark to speak at his funeral and share Jesus to his friends and family. Mark preached the gospel at George's funeral, where other family members who had witnessed a spiritual awakening in George just prior to him going home to heaven also began to ask Mark about Jesus Christ.

Didn't we see a similar event occur with Jesus when the crowds were yelling, "Crucify Him!" And what did Jesus say? "Father, forgive them, for they know not what they do" (Luke 23:34)! Wow! In exchange for our contempt toward Him, we received love, life, compassion, and salvation. In exchange for his contempt toward Jesus in Mark, George received love, life, compassion, and salvation! In exchange for Mark's contempt toward Jesus in me, Mark received love, life, compassion, salvation, and a brother forever named Ellis Lucas!

It took a broken Mark Webb and the heart of Jesus Christ to extend the life-saving love of Jesus to his former enemy. Mark was indeed a true transformed believer in Jesus Christ, as well as a genuine reflection of His likeness and a faithful and obedient follower of Him. Mark is a courageous man of God who is always willing to put everything he has on the line for an opportunity to share Jesus Christ with both friend and foe, just as Jesus before him did!

Mark had been the proverbial black sheep of his family just as I had been in mine. Moreover, we both had serious concerns when it came to trusting Christianity. We both had our share of challenges and thorns to overcome in life, and sadly, even more so after becoming Christians. But still, Mark would always make the most of every opportunity, redeeming the time and never squandering away an opportunity to share what great things God had done in his life. I witnessed God's heart for the lost and broken become Mark's heart for the lost and broken.

Not long after that, another door for evangelism opened, and I asked Mark to join us and preach the Gospel for an event in the parking lot of the Savannah Ave. Baptist Church at St. Joseph, Missouri. At that event, a young man on his way to commit suicide that night heard the music and walked about a mile just listening. And though trying to go unnoticed, he heard Mark preach the gospel and share his story, and it changed his young life forever. He committed his life to Jesus's plan and will for his life immediately following the event and later became a full-time active member of that church.

We did another event in a garage church where Mark spoke, and another troubled young man came to faith in Jesus Christ. Mark preached at a small church in Winston, Missouri, again in St. Joseph, Spearfish, South Dakota, and again at the 2013 evangelistic outreach held at the St. Joseph Civic Arena on his nine-year anniversary of being saved. Mark has served on the His Song Evangelistic Ministries board of directors and has been to various other events in Colorado and Missouri since he last spoke at a His Song outreach.

God's heart for me, however, was to do all I could within my sphere of knowledge and influence to strengthen Mark as iron would sharpen iron, and to encourage him to be all that he was created in Christ Jesus to be. At one point, there were no two people more divided than Mark Webb and myself. Could I have ever imagined the great things God had in store for Mark and me? Not in a thousand years! But again, that is what the Scriptures mean when it says, "No eye has seen, no ear has heard, and no heart has conceived of what God has prepared for those who love Him" (1 Cor. 2:9)!

I love the following quote from Mark, which captures in his own words the transforming power of God:

> I was lost—not only spiritually, but I was also lost in sickness. The worst kind of sickness was better than the best kind of dying for someone like me. Being the god of my own life was my sickness, and in my mind, there was no other god but me. In John 3:2, Nicodemus said, "Rabbi, we know that You are a teacher come from God, for no one can do these signs that You do unless God is with him." Nicodemus was honest with Jesus, confessing, "I know God is with You, but He's not with me." I was lost and dishonest with Ellis. I couldn't let him tell me there was any other God but me—a God Who loved me and could help me, heal me, and give me a new life!
>
> In John 3:3, Jesus answered Nicodemus: "Truly, truly, I say to you, unless one is born again he cannot see the kingdom of God." Like Nicodemus, I was confused and scared because I knew that God was with Ellis but wasn't with me. But that was never true, because on April 19, 2004, God made it clear that He was with me too, just as He had been with Ellis during the

dark days of his struggle before Jesus came into his life. John 3:16 says, "For God so loved the world, that He gave His only Son, that whoever believes in Him should not perish but have eternal life."

After watching the *Passion of the Christ* (by Mel Gibson), I couldn't sleep a wink for weeks from the haunting reality of what Christ had suffered because of my sickness and from realizing that I wasn't the god of anything and that if something didn't change, I was going to burn in hell! That something did happen when Christ revealed Himself to me the night of April 19, 2004, when I became a born-again Christian. My life began the day I died to myself. This was the message I was reading the morning of April 19, 2004, and a message I hope you will take to heart yourselves: "Truly, truly, I say to you, unless a grain of wheat falls into the earth and dies, it remains alone; but if it dies, it bears much fruit. Whoever loves his life loses it, and whoever hates his life in this world will keep it for eternal life. If anyone serves Me, he must follow Me; and where I am, there will My servant be also. If anyone serves Me, the Father will honor him (John 12:24–26)." (Mark Webb)

If God can do that with just two former enemies, imagine what would happen if an entire nation were to set aside their differences just for a single day and do the same? Wow! The world would never be the same!

CHAPTER 14

WHO DO MEN SAY I AM?

For more than half my natural life I lived in bondage, confused about God, confused about life, confused about death, eternity, and myself. Moreover, I was confused about why our great God and Savior, Jesus Christ, Creator of the universe, Whose power is infinite, would need to die on a cross when He could destroy Satan in one breath. Perhaps the greatest question of our time is this: "Who is Jesus Christ?" Was He just an exceptional man, or was He God in the flesh, as Peter, James, Paul, John, and His other disciples believed?

In fact, that was the very question Jesus asked when visiting the villages near Caesarea Philippi. According to Mark, they were walking along, and Jesus asked His disciples, "Who do people say I am?" (Mark 8:27). If Jesus is God, then why was it necessary for Him to die on a cross? And while I'm not a Bible scholar or a theologian, 1 Peter 1:19, Acts 20:28, and 1 Corinthians 6:19–20 say we were all purchased with a price. In fact, an important passage regarding Jesus understanding His "set apart" role in the Father's redemptive plan is Mark 10:45, in which Jesus declares that His mission not only includes sacrificing His own life but also involves giving His life as a "ransom" for many, saying that, "The Son of man came not to be ministered unto, but to minister, and to give His life a ransom for many."

But for a purchase or transaction to take place, there must be two things: a buyer and a seller. Now, so far, every commentator I have read regarding the price paid in exchange for our redemption pretty much pushed Satan out of the equation, as though he had no bearing whatsoever on this whole scenario. However, the word *redemption* in my Bible Dictionary defines this word as "Finding its context in the social, legal, and religious customs of the ancient world, the metaphor of redemption includes the ideas of losing from a bond, setting free from captivity or slavery, buying back something lost or sold, exchanging something in one's possession for something possessed by another, and ransoming."

I find it extremely difficult to understand how God became both the buyer and the seller when He is God and, under those requirements, any number of conditions could have been put in place as a means of pardoning or forgiving our sins and iniquities. For instance, if that were the case, why not allow for a simple pardon based on repentance, only without the brutality that took place when Jesus was savagely beaten beyond recognition and crucified for the sins of the world? Furthermore, why would God need to purchase something He already owns? Likewise, why is Christ's death portrayed as the payment price for the deliverance of those held captive by Satan?

According to Matthew's gospel, there was no other option. "And He [Jesus] went a little farther, and fell on His face, and prayed, saying, 'O my Father, if it be possible, let this cup pass from me: nevertheless, not as I will, but as thou wilt'" (Matt. 26:39)! It seems elementary that God would allow evil to exist in order that He may have a platform for showing His mercy, grace, and compassion. If man had never fallen, there would have been no opportunity to show divine mercy. Likewise, loving God is our prerogative; it is not a forced decision. Just as we wouldn't want to be married to someone we loved more than life itself if the other person was forced to enter the relationship, God wouldn't want that either.

But how is the body of Christ described in the New Testament? The bride of Christ. The imagery and symbolism of marriage is applied to Christ and the body of believers, known as the church. The church is comprised of those who have trusted in Jesus Christ as their personal Savior and have received eternal life. Christ, the Bridegroom, has sacrificially and lovingly chosen the church to be His bride (Eph. 5:25–27). But before the actual wedding ceremony and the consummation of the marriage, there would be an extended engagement known as a betrothal, a period in Biblical times during which the bride and groom were separated until the wedding.

Just as there was a betrothal in biblical times, so is the bride of Christ (the church) separate from her Bridegroom during the church age. Her responsibility during the betrothal period is to be faithful to Him (2 Cor. 11:2; Eph. 5:24). At the rapture, the church will be united with the Bridegroom, and the official "wedding ceremony" will take place, and the eternal union of Christ and His bride will be actualized (Rev. 19:7–9; 21:1–2).

But before a betrothal could take place, there would first be an agreed-upon price, either between the father of the groom and the father of the bride or the groom himself and the father of the bride. The price that the Groom would pay to the father of the bride was called a "mohar." "Mohar" is a masculine noun meaning "the purchase price for a bride." That's exactly what the crucifixion of Jesus Christ was—the negotiated terms agreed upon by both the buyer and the seller regarding the price He would pay for the bride He loved.

Did Jesus have to agree to those terms resulting in such vicious public humiliation and savage murder? No, He wasn't forced into any decision but instead willingly agreed to pay the price for the bride He loved and adored. He is God, and He could have dumped us like a bad habit, destroyed the universe and Satan and created for Himself a new universe and a new bride, if that's what He'd wanted to do. But unlike the paper vows and plastic promises exchanged in many marriages today that are quickly abandoned, Jesus, the Founder and Perfecter of our faith, chose to, for the joy that was set before Him, endure the cross, despising the shame, and die on a cross to be with the bride He loves.

The question is how did these terms come into existence and why? Well, thus says the Lord, "You have sold yourselves for nothing, and you shall be redeemed without money" (Isa. 52:3). But who did they sell themselves into slavery to? In John chapter eight, we find Jesus speaking to a group of Jews when the conversation suddenly turns violent. John wrote, "Then Jesus said to those Jews who believed Him, 'If you abide in My word, you are My disciples indeed.

And you shall know the truth, and the truth shall make you free.' They answered Him, 'We are Abraham's descendants, and have never been in bondage to anyone. How can You say, "You will be made free"?' Jesus answered them, 'Most assuredly, I say to you, whoever commits sin is a slave of sin. And a slave does not abide in the house forever, but a son abides forever. Therefore if the Son makes you free, you shall be free indeed'" (John 8:31–36).

This fanned the fire, and being devout Jews, they threatened to kill Him. But Jesus said to them, "If God [not Abraham] were your Father, you would love Me, for I proceeded forth and came from God; nor have I come of Myself, but He sent Me. Why do you not understand My speech? Because you are not able to listen to My word. You are of your father the devil, and the desires of your father you want to do. He was a murderer from the beginning, and does not stand in the truth, because there is no truth in him. When he speaks a lie, he speaks from his own resources, for he is a liar and the father of it" (John 8:42–44).

Jesus just made a distinction between God, the Father of the saved, and Satan, the father of the unbelieving slaves, whose minds the god of this age (Satan) has blinded, who do not believe, lest the light of the gospel of the glory of Christ, Who is the image of God, should shine on them (2 Cor. 4:4). However, since the fall in the Garden of Eden affected all people from Adam to now, separating all people from God by sin and condemning all of humanity to eternal damnation apart from a kinsmen redeemer (who both had something to offer that appealed to the slave holder and could afford to pay the price), the ball was in Satan's court. Why? Because all have sinned and fall short of the glory of God (Rom. 3:23). Moreover, the wages of sin is death, but the gift of God is eternal life in Christ Jesus our Lord (Rom. 6:23)!

Sin entered the world through one man, and death through sin, thus spreading death to all men, because all sinned (Rom. 5:12). Therefore, as through one man's offense judgment came to all men, resulting in condemnation, even so through one Man's righteous act the free gift came to all men, resulting in justification of life. For as by one man's disobedience many were made sinners, so also by one Man's obedience many will be made righteous (Rom. 5:18–19).

Nevertheless, that still doesn't answer the question of why. If humanity was the only leverage Satan had in his war against God, why would he agree to any terms that might backfire and put his very existence in jeopardy? Well, if we look at Isaiah chapter fourteen, we see a very ambitious and determined Satan making a lofty declaration when he said, "I will ascend to heaven; above the stars of God. I will set my throne on high; I will sit on the mount of assembly in the far reaches of the north; I will ascend above the heights of the clouds; I will make myself like the Most-High" (Isa. 14:13–14)!

That lofty thought got Satan cast out of heaven and undoubtedly intensified his frustration and anger toward God. In any case, "Pride goes before destruction, a haughty spirit before a fall" (Prov. 16:18). If I were in Satan's position, I would be very concerned, especially at the thought of spending eternity tormented in total darkness in a lake of fire that burns forever without end and knowing that if he didn't come up with a plan to bring down the Holy Trinity and destroy Jesus Christ, his fate was sealed.

I honestly believe it's possible that Satan may have thought he had the upper hand by holding humanity captive as a result of the fall. That could explain why Jesus temporarily set aside His deity to make Himself of no reputation, taking the form of a bondservant and coming in the likeness of men. And being found in appearance as a man, He humbled Himself and became obedient to the point of death, even the death of the cross (Phil. 2:7–8)!

Satan knew that sin had contaminated the entire human race and that the wages of sin is death (Rom. 6:23). Well, if one of the conditions was that Christ become a man, perhaps he thought sin would illuminate his archrival Jesus Christ, canceling the threat of eternal damnation. In like manner, since sin entered this world through man and not the woman, that could explain the virgin birth. If Satan didn't have a copy of Genesis then he may have been operating on the assumption that, since Eve was the first to eat of the Tree of the Knowledge of Good and Evil, sin had entered through both the man and the woman. But since sin had entered the human race only through the male and is transferred from generation to generation through our fathers, then Christ could still fulfill His end of the bargain by being born of woman who was conceived by the Holy Spirit, thereby avoiding the sin epidemic and still becoming a member of the human race.

Modern scientists have discovered that the Y chromosome is one of the two sex chromosomes in humans (the other is the X chromosome). The sex chromosomes form one of the twenty-three pairs of human chromosomes in each cell. The Y chromosome spans more than fifty-nine million building blocks of DNA and represents almost two percent of the total DNA in cells. Each person normally has one pair of sex chromosomes in each cell. The Y chromosome is present in males, who have one X and one Y chromosome, while females have two X chromosomes.

In our Lord's DNA, there would be no Y chromosomes transferred from the father to the son like there would be under normal birth circumstances, because God was His Father and Mary was still a virgin until after the birth of baby Jesus. If Satan got wind of that, perhaps that's why he waited until Christ was of age and then when He was led by the Spirit in the wilderness, Satan tempted him for forty days. The devil took him up and revealed to him all the kingdoms of the world in a moment of time. "I will give you the glory of these kingdoms and authority over them," the devil said, "because they are mine to give to anyone I please." Notice that Jesus didn't dispute Satan's claim as owner of the kingdoms of the world. Satan continued, "I will give it all to you if you will worship me." Jesus replied, "The Scriptures say, 'You must worship the Lord your God and serve only Him'" (Luke 4:1–8).

James 1:13 states that Jesus cannot be tempted because He doesn't have a sin nature, being born of a virgin. Therefore, when all else failed, perhaps Satan thought the only option he had left was to kill the Messiah. So, when Passover morning came, all the chief priests and elders of the people plotted against Jesus to put Him to death. And when they had bound Him, they led Him away and delivered Him to Pontius Pilate, the governor (Matt. 27:1–2).

According to the Bible, Jesus suffered, bled, and died that we might have life. God revealed His love for us in that, while we were yet sinners, Christ died for us (Rom. 5:8)! Moreover, according to historical accounts, Jesus, just as He predicted, was betrayed by one of His own disciples, Judas Iscariot, and was arrested. In a mock trial under the Roman governor, Pontius Pilate, Jesus was convicted of treason and condemned to die on a wooden cross. Prior to being nailed to the cross, Jesus was brutally beaten beyond recognition (Isa. 52:10). He was whipped mercilessly with a Roman cat-o'-nine-tails, a whip with bits of bone and metal that would rip flesh. He was punched repeatedly, kicked, and spat upon. Then, using mallets, the Roman executioners pounded the heavy iron nails into Jesus's wrists and feet. Then they dropped the cross in a hole in the ground between two thieves (Matt. 27:38).

At about the ninth hour, Jesus cried out with a loud voice, saying, "Eli, Eli, lema sabachthani?" which is translated, "My God, my God, why have You forsaken Me?" (Matt. 27:46). Jesus hung there for six hours. Then, at three o'clock in the afternoon—the exact same time the Passover lamb was being sacrificed as a sin offering (Exod. 12)—Jesus cried out, "It is finished," and died. Jesus had been on the cross from approximately 9:00 a.m. until 3:00 p.m., a total of six hours.

John adds the detail that Jesus's trial before Pontius Pilate was taking place, according to Roman time, "about the sixth hour" (John 19:14, ESV). Since the Romans started counting their hours at midnight, the "sixth hour" would start at 6:00 a.m.

Suddenly the sky went dark and an earthquake shook the land, terrifying the people. Pilate wanted verification that Jesus was dead before allowing His crucified body to be buried. So a Roman guard thrust a spear into Jesus's side. The mixture of blood and water that flowed out was a clear indication that Jesus was dead. Once His death was certified by the guards, Jesus's body was then taken down from the cross and buried in Joseph of Arimathea's tomb. Next, the Roman guards sealed the tomb and secured it with a twenty-four-hour watch.

However, after Christ's resurrection, when the tomb was found empty, the Jewish leaders were stunned. They accused the disciples of stealing Jesus's body. But the Romans had assigned a twenty-four-hour watch at the tomb with a trained guard unit made up of four to sixteen soldiers. Josh McDowell notes that these were not ordinary soldiers. "When that guard unit failed in its duty—if they fell asleep, left their position, or failed in any way—there are a number of historical sources that go back and describe what happens. Many of them are stripped of their own clothes, they are burned alive in a fire started with their own garments or they are crucified upside down. The Roman Guard unit was especially committed to discipline and they feared failure in any and every way."

It would have been impossible for anyone to have slipped by the Roman guards and moved a two-ton stone. Yet the stone was moved away and the body of Jesus was missing. Something beyond extraordinary must have happened for the followers of Jesus who loved and adored Him so much to have ceased mourning, ceased hiding, and began fearlessly proclaiming that they had seen Jesus alive. Each eyewitness account reports that Jesus suddenly appeared bodily to His followers, first appearing to the women. Later, according to the eyewitness accounts, all the disciples saw Jesus on more than ten separate occasions. They wrote that He showed them His hands and feet and told them to touch Him. And He reportedly ate with them and later appeared alive to more than five hundred followers on one occasion.

Peter told a crowd in Caesarea why he and the other disciples were so convinced Jesus was alive. "We apostles are witnesses of all He did throughout Israel and in Jerusalem. They put Him to death by crucifying Him, but God raised Him to life three days later. What's more, we were those who ate and drank with Him after He rose from the dead" (Acts 10:39–41)! Well, that would certainly dry up a lot of tears in a hurry and cause their cups to overflow with joy.

So, who is Jesus Christ? He is the one Who formed you and redeemed you and then called you by your name (Isa. 43:1). Jesus

Christ is the only person to fulfill the following prophecies and meet all the detailed specifications that only the Messiah could meet:

- His lineage would come from David [Jer. 23:5] (600 BC).
- His birth would occur in Bethlehem (Micah 5:2).
- "You, O Bethlehem Ephrathah, are only a small village in Judah. Yet a ruler of Israel will come from you, one Whose origins are from the distant past" (Micah 5:2, NLT).
- "The Lord Himself will choose [a] sign. Look! The virgin will conceive a child! She will give birth to a son and will call Him Immanuel, meaning 'God is with us'" (Isa. 7:14, NLT).
- He would migrate to Egypt (Hos. 11:1).
- He would live in Nazareth (Isa. 11:1).
- The Messiah would be betrayed for thirty pieces of silver [Zech. 11:13] (487 BC).
- "They gave him thirty pieces of silver" [Matt. 26:15] (30 AD).
- Prophecy: The Messiah would have His hands and feet pierced [Ps. 22:16] (1000 BC). Fulfillment: "They came to a place called The Skull. All three were crucified there— Jesus on the center cross, and the two criminals on either side" [Luke 23:33] (30 AD).
- Prophecy: People would cast lots for the Messiah's clothing [Ps. 22:18] (1000 BC). Fulfillment: "The soldiers...took His robe, but it was seamless, woven in one piece from the top. So they said, 'Let's not tear it but throw dice to see who gets it'" [John 19:23–24] (30 AD).
- The Messiah would appear riding on a donkey [Zech. 9:9] (500 BC). Fulfillment: "They brought the animals to Him and threw their garments over the colt, and He sat on it" [Matt. 21:7] (30 AD).
- A messenger would be sent to herald the Messiah [Mal. 3:1] (500 BC). Fulfillment: John told them, "I baptize with water, but right here in the crowd is someone you do not know" [John 1:26] (27 AD).

These are only a short list of well over a hundred prophecies already fulfilled by Jesus Christ and none other. These are now part of world history rather than a futuristic or revolutionary list of imaginary fantasies, as today's postmodernist might suggest. Jesus Christ is the Creator and Redeemer of the world and the absolute one and only door that enters into heaven! But the question remains, "Who is the Jesus of the Bible to you?"

CHAPTER 15

THE SPIRIT AND THE BRIDE SAY, "COME."

I recently wrote a song specifically for the lost, broken, and hurting people of this unforgiving world—a theme song titled "Wanted" for our live Wanted events! The lyrics, which were inspired by Psalm 139, read, "I'm wanted, and there's no place I can go away from Your Spirit. Wanted, there's nowhere I can flee away from Your presence. Should I ascend up into heaven, or go down to the fire below, You've got me surrounded with Your love!"

The point is this: there is nowhere you or I can go to escape the relentless pursuit of Christ's redeeming love. "Come to Me, all who are weary and heavy-laden, and I will give you rest" (Matt. 11:28). The question is "Where do you want to spend eternity?" It took me losing my life on March 6, 1997, to find it when Jesus Christ wrote these words on the tablets of my heart: "Ellis, I love you, and I'm here for you! I know your situation, and, Ellis, I am concerned for you! Ellis, I can help. If you will commit your life to Me today, at this very hour, and trust Me, I will forgive, heal, and restore your broken life!"

All my tomorrows had run out, but by the loving grace of Christ Jesus, I was fortunate to be given a final opportunity to decide which destiny I would choose. Jesus told His disciples, "I am the way, the truth, and the life. No one comes to the Father except through Me" (John 14:6). This is the most important decision you will ever have to make. This verse is so precious and meaningful to me, especially when it was Jesus Christ Who brought me the good news!

"How beautiful upon the mountains are the feet of him who brings good news, who proclaims peace, who brings glad tidings of good things, who proclaims salvation, who says to Zion, 'Your God reigns!'" The writer of the book of Hebrews wrote, "Since therefore it remains that some must enter it, and those to whom it was first preached did not enter because of disobedience, again He designates a certain day, saying, 'Today,' after such a long time, as it has been said, 'Today, if you hear His voice, do not harden your hearts'" (Heb. 4:6–7)!

Now is the acceptable time; today is the day of salvation. Tomorrow's not promised to anyone. If you would like to receive the gift of eternal life, you must believe in the Lord Jesus Christ and that He died to pay the penalty for your sins and that God raised Him from the dead on the third day. You must both acknowledge your sins and ask that they be forgiven and then put your trust in Him and, with His help, be fully committed to the repentance of your sins. This simply means to turn away from your sin and to Jesus Christ (Acts 3:19).

John said we can be absolutely sure that we have eternal life:

> I write these things to you who believe in the name of the Son of God, that you may know that you have eternal life. And this is the confidence that we have toward Him, that if we ask anything according to His will He hears us. And if we know that He hears us in whatever we ask, we know that we have the requests that we have asked of Him. (1 John 5:13–15)
>
> His divine power has granted to us all things that pertain to life and godliness, through the knowledge of Him Who called us to His own glory and excellence, by which He has also granted to us His precious, unbreakable, and very great promises, so that through them we may become partakers of the divine nature, having escaped from the corruption that is in the world because of sinful desire. For this very reason, make every

effort to supplement your faith with virtue, and virtue with knowledge, and knowledge with self-control, and self-control with steadfastness, and steadfastness with godliness, and godliness with brotherly affection, and brotherly affection with love. (2 Pet. 1:3–7)

Be all the more diligent to confirm your calling and election, for if you practice these qualities you will never fall. For in this way there will be richly provided for you a glorious and highly anticipated entrance into the eternal kingdom of our Lord and Savior Jesus Christ. (2 Pet. 1:10–11)!

That includes eternal life in heaven and a purpose-filled life here on earth. It includes meaningful relationships with genuine Christ-centered love that bears all things, believes all things, hopes all things, and endures all things (1 Cor. 13:7).

John 14:6 says that there is no other way to heaven except through Jesus Christ. Therefore, "Enter by the narrow gate; for wide is the gate and broad is the way that leads to destruction, and there are many who go in by it. Because narrow is the gate and difficult is the way which leads to life, and there are few who find it" (Matt. 7:13–14)! And finally, "Blessed are those who wash their robes, so that they may have the right to the tree of life and that they may enter the city by the gates. Outside are the dogs and sorcerers and the sexually immoral and murderers and idolaters, and everyone who loves and practices falsehood. 'I, Jesus, have sent my angel to testify to you about these things for the churches. I am the root and the descendant of David, the bright morning star.' The Spirit and the Bride say, 'Come.' And let the one who hears say, 'Come.' And let the one who is thirsty come; let the one who desires take the water of life without price" (Rev. 22:14–17)!

- Mark 2:17 – Jesus said He did not come to call the righteous, but sinners, to repentance.

- John 3:16 – God so loved the whole world that He gave His only begotten Son, that whoever believes in Him should not perish but have everlasting life.
- Romans 3:23 – All have sinned and fallen short of the glory of God.
- Romans 6:23 – The wages of sin is death, but the gift of God is eternal life in Christ Jesus our Lord.
- Ephesians 2:8-9 – For by grace you have been saved through faith; and that not of yourselves, it is the gift of God; not as a result of works, so that no one may boast.
- Romans 10:9 – If you confess with your mouth the Lord Jesus and believe in your heart that God has raised Him from the dead, you will be saved.
- 1 John 5:13 – These things I have written to you who believe in the name of the Son of God, in order that you may know that you have eternal life.
- 1 John 1:9 – If we confess our sins, He is faithful and righteous to forgive us our sins and to cleanse us from all unrighteousness.

The Prayer of David. If you want to begin your personal relationship with Jesus Christ, you can begin like this:

> Have mercy upon me, O God, according to Your lovingkindness; according to the multitude of Your tender mercies, blot out my transgressions. Wash me thoroughly from my iniquity, and cleanse me from my sin. For I acknowledge my transgressions, and my sin is always before me. Against You and You alone have I sinned, and done this evil in Your sight, that You may be found just when You speak and blameless when You judge. Behold, I was brought forth in iniquity, and in sin my mother conceived me. Behold, You desire truth in the inward parts, and in the hidden part You will make me to know wisdom.

Purge me with hyssop, and I shall be clean; wash me, and I shall be whiter than snow. Make me hear joy and gladness, that the bones [spirit and heart] You have broken may rejoice. Hide Your face from my sins, and blot out all my iniquities. Create in me a clean heart, O God, and renew a steadfast spirit within me. Do not cast me away from Your presence, and do not take Your Holy Spirit from me. Father, please send Jesus Christ, Your only begotten Son, Who gave His life on a cross as a propitiation for my sins, and restore to me the joy of Your salvation, and uphold me by Your generous Spirit (Ps. 51:1–12)

Amen!

If you are receiving Jesus Christ for the first time, then I want to be the first to welcome you to the family of God. Also, please contact us at either of the web addresses listed below and let us know how we can pray for you. Find a good Bible-believing, Bible-teaching church, and if you're not sure where to start, we will help you find a church in your area to help you grow in your walk with Jesus Christ. Be sure to read your Bible, and when you contact us, I will send you a copy of *Welcome to the Family of God* by Sandy Adams, a powerful new-believer's booklet that will help you onto the right track toward heaven!

Thank you also for taking the time to read this book. I hope it has awakened your spirit and blessed your heart. And finally, we would love to see you at a live Wanted event and meet you in person, Lord willing. But for now, God bless, and our best to you all!

www.ellislucas.com

www.hisheartunited.org

ABOUT THE AUTHOR

The life of someone like Ellis Lucas usually doesn't get written in books—instead, it's "written" on the garbage heaps and junk piles of blighted urban areas—the saddest parts of our cities which record the tales of those who've totally given up to alcoholism, defeat, drug addiction, rejection, and a whole lot more, but not Ellis Lucas. "If ever I have seen a sinner, sprinting headlong toward destruction, transformed by Christ into a wonderful life of service to the glory of God, Ellis Lucas is that man!" (Rick Simbro).

Ellis Lucas is the author of a powerful biographical series, a songwriter and recording artist, recently recording three original songs with members of Kelly Clarkson's and Mandisa's bands and is the president of His Heart United, a Missouri and Colorado 501(c)(3) not-for-profit ministry. Nevertheless, for twenty-four years, drug and alcohol addictions progressively ruined Ellis's life so thoroughly that even Ellis believed there was no conceivable way of recovering enough to live a normal life ever again. Yet as it is written: "If our hearts condemn us, God is greater than our hearts and knows everything" (1 John 3:20)!

Ellis's autobiography *The Potter and the Clay* has been adopted for use in prisons, county jails, rehab centers, and rescue missions in Colorado, Kansas, Missouri, Arizona, Pennsylvania, Florida, Minnesota, and Alabama and continues to expand with books to be donated to various programs in additional states. Ellis has been a guest on the Herman and Sharron show on CTN the Christian Television Network, *The Harvest Show* on Lesea Broadcasting, Real Life, Cornerstone Television Network, Devin Thorpe, Your Mark on the World, Messiah Community Talk Radio with Michael Lorin, and recently did a two-hour interview with Michael Rasnick of the 700 Club.

Ellis has been interviewed by local television news shows, newspapers, and radio broadcasts, both Christian and secular shows in Missouri, Colorado, and South Dakota. Interviews regarding His Heart United live outreach events that took place at the Black Hills State University in South Dakota, and prestigious venues in Missouri and Colorado including the Douglas County Fair Grounds in Castle Rock, Colorado. Ellis's story was also featured on "Unshackled," an outreach ministry of Moody Radio and Pacific Garden Missions located in Chicago, Illinois, and was heard all over the world in fourteen different languages.

Today, Ellis travels the country speaking at churches, prisons and jails, rescue missions and special outreach events like the Sturgis, South Dakota motorcycle rally where Ellis is scheduled to headline the Light Up the Hills rally, hosted by the Fellowship of Motorcycle Ministries for two nights during the 2019 rally. Ellis has spent the past several years organizing evangelistic outreach events for churches as well as two- and three-day His Heart United city-wide evangelistic events. Ellis's life is a demonstration of God's redeeming power and love toward all of humanity and as a devout Christian and committed follower of Jesus Christ, Ellis's life, in essence, has become a gift to life itself as an inspiration to broken lives the world over.

Born in Cameron, Missouri, Ellis Lucas lives in Colorado Springs, Colorado, with his wife Peggi Sue, the inspiration behind Ellis becoming an author and the founding of His Heart United Network of Christian Ministries. For more information about Ellis, visit www.HisHeartUnited.org or www.ellislucas.com. Your heart will be better for it.

Ellis Lucas on Unshackled:

https://unshackled.org/program/ellis-lucas-pt-1/
https://unshackled.org/program/ellis-lucas-pt-2/

Peggi Lucas on Unshackled:

https://unshackled.org/program/peggi-lucas/

Made in the USA
San Bernardino,
CA